Hugh Harmon

Worthy Art Thou

By
Hugh Harmon

Hugh Harmon

Published in the United States by: Kingdom Book and Gift LLP an imprint of *Love Fellowship Kingdom Restoration Tabernacle*, Columbia, SC

Distributed in the United States by: Kingdom Book and Gift LLP, P.O. Box 291975, Columbia, SC 29229 * www.kingdombookandgift.com Email: kingdombookgift@aol.com

First published by Kingdom Book and Gift LLP 06/28/2007

ISBN: 978-0-6151-5281-3

This book is dedicated to my two precious daughters, Inaya Renea and Chai-Soleil.

I thank God for each one of you.
You are worthy and precious gifts to us all!
The Bible says that every good and perfect gift comes from the Lord.
May God continue to bring blessings into my life directly because of you.
Always remember that Jesus is Number One, and that He is your first Father.

Table of Contents

Worthy Art Thou
By Hugh J. Harmon

Foreword

Have you ever thought of how much God was worth? Have you ever hazarded a guess of how much you are worth? The idea of calculating the worth of God is one that may be accounted as sacrilegious. Man attempting to assign a value to the person of God, think of it, what a travesty! But this is a sentiment that is ever before the eyes of a suffering saint. How much is your belief in God worth? Is it worth enough for you to face persecution, victimization, targeting for assault and affliction? Many who have died for God's sake and who may have endured the life of martyrdom would gladly answer that it is worth much more than life itself, more than life itself.

Let's not forget the question of how much you are worth. This is a question, a figure that one may never invest thought unless you were faced with the experience or likelihood of kidnap for ransom. How much would the kidnappers ask for you in ransom? If we were to use the economists or the accountants' formulas for calculating worth many of us would come up literally bankrupt. What therefore can we be worth given our corruptible nature? What worth is there to be found in a being that treads the line of life and death, subject to natures perils, only able to depend on chance occurrences when it comes to predicting our future steps? What worth is there in being a higher form of mortal flesh that has been assigned a date of expiration?

Wise King Solomon at the close of his reign brocaded in riches and steeped with accolades concerning his intellectual profundity utters:

What profit hath a man of all his labor which he taketh under the sun.

> **Ecclesiastes 1:3 KJV**

7

How could a man so blessed as Solomon so rewarded in wealth and fame find life such a vain pursuit? He had the riches and the wisdom. His possessions and bank of knowledge was and still is unparalleled among men, and yet still he came to the grave conclusion that much of life was vain empty pursuit. This vain unsubstantial pursuit is what makes the question of the worth of man so profound and critical.

Each and every Sunday in this and many other Judeo-Christian nations throughout the world one can be sure to hear the Words, "God is worthy to be praised!" uttered either in concert by a congregation of believers or by the individual preacher. It may come from the pews, or from the choir stalls. It may come from a bowed head on bent knees or from a head raised heavenward with outstretched arms. Regardless of the source, the testament of the size and share number of people worldwide who consider themselves Christian or count themselves as part of the Body of Christ, it speaks volumes of the worth that is to be found in the Carpenter of Galilee.

I can't recall the first time I ever heard about him. But I do remember the reverence and sincerity with which he was talked about for as long as I could remember. It might have been in a bedtime story from my grandmother, a Bible reading at Eucharist on Sunday morning or during a class at Sunday School, when I first heard of Jesus of Nazareth, or of Jesus the carpenter from Galilee. The stories were always the same, this man of no repute, reserved in appearance, outspoken in his kindness to everyone (especially the young and needy) and ready and able to help to make the lives of others more promising. It was automatic you could almost predict the outcomes were going to be dramatic, miraculous even. Blind men came and left seeing for the first time. Deaf people experienced a flood of sound that was new to their old ears, they could finally hear. Men, women and children lame, afflicted, broken and bleeding encountered this man and were cured and made whole. Some men, young, rebellious, hated and looked down upon, twelve to be exact in the space of three years were elevated to states of spiritual authority that they themselves would never have imagined just by being in his company, and heeding his counsel.

Even to my delicate, young mind I could tell that this man, if the stories were true was worthy of all the accolades that were heaped upon him. From Genesis to the Gospels we are given a distinctive account of how God's purposeful plan for mankind included the reconciliation of man unto Him through the redemptive work of his Son, Jesus Christ. From the Gospels to Revelation, the final stage of God's master plan is scripted. The calling out of the Church, the body of Christ, derived from the remnant of believers in whom Christ's Spirit is shed abroad among. The separation of unbelievers to eternal torment is the conclusion of the body of his Word. Throughout this account the worth of God to every believer is clear and outstanding, but the worth of man to God is a bit less clear and concise. In fact we have to many times imply what our worth is to God.

In this book, I have taken the bold step after much prayer and with much heavenly inspiration to write about the worth of God to us and about our worth to Him. "Worthy Art Thou..." is an accumulation of study notes and a series of sermons on the topic of human worthiness and God's worthiness. The worth of God is an insurmountable figure. For me to attempt to speak as though I know everything about God's worth to us would be to do that faculty of study and theology an injustice. It would be, as it were, *'biting off more than I could chew'*. I cannot attempt to cover all the aspects of God's worth but I will assay to write on what God leads me to discuss. And in writing about what we as human's are worth I can only write from personal experience, from what I have gathered in the way of counsel from colleagues, friends and foes, and from what the Word of God has said on the topic. This is what I have endeavored to do.

Worth is a 'weighted' term in both the literal and the figurative sense of its use. It is a term that denotes subjectivity, and a judgment call. What I consider to be of worth, may not be worth anything to someone else. By what standard of worth are we working with anyway? When we decide the standard, then we can determine the universality of our subjective summation. As Christians our standard should be God's word. His Word says that I am worth something to Him, what is that? God's word also proclaims and actively infers that He is worth a great deal to us. May this study of God's worth and of your worth, give you hope to transcend all your doubts and misgivings of the value of this life, and give you a resolve to continue to fight the good fight of faith.

**According as he hath chosen us in him
before the foundation of the world, that we should be
holy and without blame before him in love:
Having predestinated us unto the adoption
of children by Jesus Christ himself
according to the good pleasure of his will.
To the praise of the glory of his grace,
wherein he hath made us accepted in the
beloved.**

Ephesians 1: 4-6 KJV

1.

The Theory of Inherent Value

The Bible gives no indication of the origin of God. It opens with the account of the beginning of life and of the sudden incursion of sin and life's ultimate ruin as a result of sin. Despite the detail that is given for the beginnings of the heavens, the earth, plants, animals and the human species we are precluded from any speculation on the beginning of God. So, where did He come from?

Let's start with what's predicated by the title of this chapter, the theory of inherent value. Worth of a thing is often times correlated to the origin of that thing, and this is what my theory of inherent value suggests. Look around you at any store catalog or just browse around in any upscale department store. A rug is usually of very little worth or value until one realizes that it is of Persian origin. Shoppers peruse aisles of clothing, accessories and household products many times making their decision to purchase not so much on listed price but on the manufacturer's tag. Made in America or made in Japan can many times be a point of decision for many a shopper. European cars for many years were believed to be of greater worth than American made or Asian-made vehicles. Even ladies shoes and accessories from certain parts of the world are considered of greater worth than from other places. Man has developed a system of standards by which they attach worth based on the subjective rubric of place of manufacture. So what if we used that same standard to determine God's worth?

Searching God's worth based on theory of inherent value would definitely depend on us having the material and information necessary to investigate God's place of manufacture. To find the place of manufacture of a toy or an automobile is an easy task because all we would have to do is find the inscription tag indicating the maker. However, to find the place of manufacture of God or essentially His origin we would have to find the same inscription and that inscription does not exist. The only place that we could possibly find even something close to that would be the Bible, which is accepted to be His inerrant and inspired Word. The Bible is His Word, therefore we could depend on Him somewhere in His Word speaking about where He came from. Most objects, items, persons or things that exist in this world either verbally speak of their origin or give physical indications in their features as to their origin, but God doesn't.

God doesn't have an origin. He doesn't give an indication of an origin. An origin cannot even be inferred from what is written in the Bible. We can conclude that God's origin is unsearchable. It is not that the layers of history from which we would have to peel are immense but rather that there is no history that exists from which to conject an opinion. The Bible is silent when it comes to discussion of the where of God, or the when of God. Where suggests that there is a space within which at one time God existed and when suggests that there is a time within which at one time God existed but we know that this is impossible. This is impossible to determine because God is omnipresent therefore there is no*where* that he could have been limited to being in. We also know that God is eternal meaning that he does not, did not and cannot be limited by the confines of time. God has no end and He had no beginning. His existence stretches from time eternal past to time infinite future.

Theologians, scientist and sociologist alike have for centuries conjectured on the origin of God. This is not, I dare say, a new endeavor but rather has been a project of man from the early days of philosophical wrangling. In these debates ideas about God being a concept created in the minds of men was always a definition that stood out. God was considered a concept created by man to explain the unexplainable. He was a concept created to weave purpose and tragedy into the patchwork quilt of life. They believed that man looking to find a first cause of all things and trying to establish the idea of order to what was becoming a chaotic state of being, created God.

Staying with our theory of inherent value, if this idea of God as a mental construct of man were true, what value then can be placed in Him. If we put value or worth in things according to their origin what worth would a God birthed in our imaginations have? A mere *poof*, a wavering in mindset would then render Him nonexistent. It is impossible to prove either way you look at it, if we use our limited intellect. Our accumulated knowledge (i.e. Science) falls short of discovering all that we can about God. When we try to determine the origin of God we can compare ourselves to computers trying to determine the origin of the programmer. God was the first computer programmer, and after creating us, He programmed us. As it is impossible for a computer to figure out its programmer so it is with man trying to figure out God. At this conclusion, I know that I will still draw opposition that is why atheist still exist today, that is why society is such a mixture of belief systems with regard to the nature of God. However, we must always present the standard and the point of view from which we draw all our conclusions. And in this case I draw my conclusions from my faith in the Word of God. The line for me must be drawn in the pages of the Bible.

> **All scripture is given by inspiration of God and is profitable for doctrine, for reproof, for correction, for instruction in righteousness:........ I charge thee therefore to...Preach the word;**
> **2 Timothy 3:16,4:1a, 2a KJV**

As we search God's origin we have to work with a clear standard, rubric or precedent in mind. The scientist is seeking clear empirical proof to come to his conclusions about God and the sociologist is seeking societal mores, ethics and belief systems that support their conclusions. In my endeavor I am working with the standard that says that the Bible is the final authority on who God is and his character. The world would have us to believe that there are no absolutes, and that everything around us is immersed in a sea of relativity. It says that reality is relative, God is relative and that truth and justice is relative. When I consider these ideas I am led to express the familiar mantra, "If you stand for nothing, you'll fall for anything...". Relativity, which is often referred to as existentialism, leads to a society of people who don't know what to believe in, and have no ground to stand on. This leads to a people who just live life determined to look out for self and opposed to anything that disrupts their pursuit of self-gratification. So we see the difficulty in purporting a theory of inherent value. It can only work if we are all looking at the same principles when it comes to determining value.

What about Jesus?

In the beginning was the Word, and the Word was with God, and the Word was God.
And the Word was made flesh, and dwelt among us...
St. John 1:1,14 KJV

Using the Bible and the scripture that is written within as a standard we cannot look at the origin of God without venturing an examination of what the Bible considers to be the incarnation of God, Jesus Christ. There is debate even among believers (i.e. among those who use the Bible as their standard) about the relationship between God the Father and God the Son. I do not wish to engender further debate at this juncture so I will not venture to add to the fracas but rather I will stick to the focus of finding out God's worth. The Bible in the New Testament draws a clear close relationship in divinity between the creator God of Genesis and Jesus of the Gospels. Jesus is referred to repeatedly as the Son of the divine, the only begotten one of the Father. Hence, this assigns a level of God status to him that to me is

incontrovertible but can be debated at the highest echelons
of theological discourse. To map the origin of God the
creator might be difficult but if we were to map the origin of
his Son we may get a better picture of God's worth. God had
no beginning but his believed son had a beginning, and even
a birth that is repeatedly referred to and is even validated by
historical evidence. There is repeated prophetic references
made to him and all the experiences and even the judicial
standard under which the people of the Bible conducted
their lives seemed to point to him. So where should we
begin? What about Jesus can give us an indication of God's
worth?

If we were to run a background check on Jesus the
information would be startling. The names, characters, and
places that we would encounter in retracing his heritage
would be at all standards disturbing and sometimes even
disappointing. Lowly beginnings, felonious characters, and
deceptive behavior are among some of the description that
we would find in the elements of his family tree. Jesus in his
celestial journey from the right hand of his Father from glory
to God man was one of embarking from a place of supreme
greatness and to a place of mediocrity. He moved from a
place where he had to surrender power to a place where he
would be subjected to humility. The son of God was born to
a poor virgin who was betrothed to a simple carpenter and
the moment of birth was in the unheralded squalor of a
manger. It all took place in a little known part of the world,
figuratively miles from the lap of luxury that one would
imagine would be the lot of divine royalty. Jesus' story was
one that many of us would be ashamed to tell friends or
associates. If it were our story we would be ashamed to tell
of the prostitute that you were related to, or of the liars and
deceivers and even murderers that were prominent members
of my lineage. Our inherent value would be stunted if we
were to relate that we were blood relatives of the town harlot,
or the adulterous king or the deceiving twin who stole his
brother's birthright and blessing. It would be devalued even

more if we let others know that we were born, and grew up in the ghetto, living in low-income housing.

God gives very little indication of where He came from. That just shows of how little value that element is of his divinity. God could have chosen any family. He could have chosen a family with much closer ties to the royalty of that time. But God chose a group of people who at first glance had checkered pasts. We can clearly state that Jesus was born of Mary, a virgin, because prophecy had to be fulfilled. We can also assert that the ancestors from whose family descended had great significance in the eyes of God, people like King David, Ruth, and Isaac. But why do we have the others? Why the Rahabs and the Jacobs? Why did they have to be interspersed among his line? These people who lived less than totally righteous lives. God was giving us insight into how we should see our own story and ourselves.

The family, in which we find ourselves, governs many times, the way we rate our self-worth. We look around our homes, we look at the people who come by and call themselves Uncle, Aunt, Cousin and we develop a sense of shame for family and eventually for ourselves. We look at the things they did or do, and we look at the consequences of that on our lives. We end up blaming family, blaming parents, blaming relatives for the difficulties we face with relationships, in our school life and in our work life. In spite of Jesus' family problems their shady backgrounds and their affiliations with the lower caste of society He still became everything He was intended to be. His worth when it was all said and done was immeasurable. Consider the honor that was bestowed on Him even as a child; shepherds from the field, royalty from the Far East all coming to see this poor child that was born in a manger in lowly Bethlehem.

How about man?

And God said, Let us make man in our image, after our likeness:
Genesis 1:26 KJV

These words give light to the thoughts of God regarding man at the very beginning. How many of you know that everything is created twice? It is first created in the mind, and then it is created in reality. Therefore, man was created twice, first in the mind of God and then in the reality of His creative will. So, this leads us to conclude that our origin can be traced to the thoughts of God. In the Bible especially in the book of Genesis we are introduced to a God who is about completing a deliberate work. God, the creator, is never double-minded. He does not overtly debate about a thought. His thoughts are conjoined to his words, and his words to his actions. God spoke and it was done automatically. God thought, spoke and it came to pass and it was good. God made no mistakes and makes no mistakes.

As we said before the world we live in gives much credence to tribal affiliations, genealogical connections and ancestral origins. The farther back in time that one could authenticate their familial heritage the greater significance is assigned to ones lineage. Unfortunately this dependence on familial links can as we said before lead some to feel as it were, worthless. We looked at the example of Jesus and his humble beginnings and the detailed genealogy that is given of him through his earthly parents. We can also look at the example of most African Americans who trace their ancestry to familial roots established in Southern United States. Deliberate efforts to dissolve familial bonds among the African slave population of pre-Civil War America essentially created a class of people in American society in post-Civil War America who had obscure origins. Many of the former slaves couldn't even use their names to trace back origin because these were usually names given by the slave master and indicated ownership and not birth affiliation. This dissolution of bonds was only the beginning of the measures that sought to relegate these people to very much a tribe of unknown origin. Legislative measures that led to slaves and descendants of slaves to be counted as two-thirds of a human being again subtracted worth from men.

Looking for worth in the things of man, in birthright, in place of birth, in clan affiliation are all factors that really and truly do not increase or add to your worth. We may be descended from the ancient Anglo-Saxon clans, East or Western Africa, Southeast Asia or from the pre-colonial Americas but does it make us more or less worthy. No, our worth is not to be found in the eyes of men but in the eyes of God.

From dust we came, and from dust we shall return, that's what the Bible says about this shell that we call a body. When we consider that we are born of the dust we really and truly subtract much of the worth that we once had placed in our beautifully built bodies. We know that we are fearfully and wonderfully made but even that assertion loses conviction once we hit the age of sagging skin and wrinkles. So, if worth isn't to be found in our physical and if it is not to be found in our origins then where is it to be found? Our worth is to found in our purpose. God had a plan when he made you.

For whom he did foreknow, he also did predestinate...
Romans 8:29a KJV

Our purpose is tied up in His will. A thing is worth to you only what it is to you and what it can do for you. Take currency as an example. Why is the US dollar worth more than the Mexican peso in America? It is not because of its origin but it is more because of what the dollar can do verses what the peso cannot do. Yes, the origin of the two forms of currency plays a part but of utmost importance is whether you can complete your transaction of purchase with one or the other. Our worth in the eyes of fellow men also comes down basically to what we can do for them. A lifeguard is of utmost importance to a drowning person, like a good lawyer is to a convicted felon, and a doctor to a critically ill patient. Our worth is to be found in our purpose, not our purpose in the eyes of men but our purpose as in the plan of God.

If man's worth is to be found in his God given purpose, what then is God's worth to us based on? As unsearchable as God's origin is, so too is His worth in totality. God is worth so much more to man and everything that makes its shadow to fall on this earth that we could even assay to research. As we take a snapshot of what God is worth to us we have to understand that it is because of God that we are able to be. It is because of him that we make our entry into this space of existence. It is because of Him that we are able to breathe, to operate, to dream, to build and to destroy. It is because of God that we have sustained good health or prosperity and wealth. It is because of him that we are able to boast and brag of what we possess, or what we intend to possess. God's worth is priceless, unmatched by any monetary figure that man could accumulate even collectively. His worth cannot be found in his origin, it cannot be found in his beginnings because He has none. God's worth is evident in life itself, in its benefits and its abundance. God is worthy.

2.

Lift Up Your Head

But thou, O Lord, art a shield for me; my glory, and the lifter of mine head.

Psalm 3:3

"He is the lifter of mine head". What a profound statement by the psalmist, a word of encouragement to anyone that feels downtrodden or overburdened by the confluence of life. A bowed head usually symbolizes a demeanor of low esteem or stature. David, the psalmist in penning this soliloquy queries God about his seeming misfortune in the face of his enemies. For many of us a God that lifts our heads is needed due to the depressing nature of the life happening around us.

A God that lifts your head is a God that empowers, rather than overpowers. David needed empowerment at this stage in his life. It wasn't about rewards because David was already guaranteed the wealth, riches and the power. He had been anointed to be king it was a done deal. David needed encouragement. Some of us just need encouragement. Encouragement through a lifted head can be of greater value to a depressed spirit than a large quantity of cash. Look at the examples of the clinically depressed millionaires and mega-stars that inundate the media and garner much attention from screaming maniacal fans. These people are many times in a catch 22. They have the wealth and the fame. That means that they have both the resources and the recognition but they are still depressed. Many of us are "minor-stars" that have some measure of provision and recognition among our peers. Some of us count ourselves as the social elite and others of us consider ourselves "well-off", however, we too also lack the common denominator and that lack pushes us to a posture of bent heads and burning shoulders.

We misconstrue the problem and deliberately pursue success in our careers, misguidedly thinking that we have not achieved enough yet and that is why we are still unhappy. Sometimes we subconsciously drown ourselves in reports and late night research to keep our minds off of the lack that we are feeling. If I keep my mind occupied on work then I will have no time to contemplate what I truly am missing.

The accolades that we achieve at work continue to pour in and the demerits that we had begun to accrue at home start to accumulate. Many of societies broken families are as a result of this area of lack and the misguided steps that we take in ratifying the problem. The answer is not in a higher salary and greater responsibility on your job. It is a much more fundamental problem that needs immediate attention or that will eventually cost you that very job to which one believes their sustenance is attached.

Who hath saved us, and called us with an holy calling, not according to our works, but according to his own purpose and grace.
2 Timothy 1:9

One of the greatest revelations that I have ever received concerning the purpose of our lives when it comes to work is the fact that the highest reward for a man's work is not what he gets for it, but what he becomes by it. Salaries, wages and income never seem to meet the mark with regard to our needs and wants. Debt to income ratio of the majority of the world's population especially in developing nations is usually unevenly bent towards a surplus in debt.

Hence, we have a flourishing industry developed in the area of assigning credit to individuals who are logically incapable of ever repaying the debt loaned to them. Credit is assayed to people who are unable to pay the full amount up front, and they are also penalized for repayment of a debt before the contractual period is completed. So we see that we really can never be truly paid for the work that we do in this life. The reward or the benefit that one should therefore look for from life must lie somewhere else. What are the things that affect life? What are the issues that play a role in shaping our lives?

As clay is molded, spun on a wheel and heated in a kiln to form a finished piece of pottery, so too are our lives worked and shaped into a finished vessel. The only contrast however is that clay is unresponsive. It is a passive receptor of all the potters handling. Human beings however, are not passive receptors but rather play an active role in positioning themselves to be molded into shape. Life doesn't happen to us as with clay, it actually happens through us. Accountability starts with us.

The question of worth leads me to analyze the paradigm of our ordinary lives being shaped by an extraordinary purpose. The idea of human worth can be expunged from the concept that if our lives were worthless God wouldn't have desired to implant us with an assignment in his overarching eternal plan for mankind. Salvation and eternal life are considered the rewards of belief in Jesus Christ as Lord. But are our lives simply strategically designed so that we come to believe in Jesus Christ as Lord and then wait to be caught up to heaven? Or are we just to shoot to get to heaven?

Theological discourse fluctuates with regard to whether gaining salvation through Jesus Christ, and being accepted into heaven is the final step. Some hold to the contention that there are levels of reward in heaven depending on the degree of spiritual attainment here in this life. Others say that regardless of one's believed spiritual stature in this life we will all occupy the same exalted station in heaven. Is it enough just to believe and sit with the guarantee of an after life? Are we not called to do anything else?

Martin Luther King once said "If a man stands for nothing he will fall for anything!" He was speaking on the concept of living life with a purpose, living life with an established standard, living life with a passionate desire to achieve certain goals, and living life with a foundational belief at heart that your living counts for something. Someone else once said that it would be a shame to live life and then find out at the end of it all that it was lived in vain. He called it "Vanity of vanities". That was how Solomon described the irony of a wasted life in the book of Ecclesiastes in the bible. Solomon wrote throughout that text with the objective of delving into what I would like to refer to as the "meat and bones" of life. He asked the searching questions that at first glance seem somewhat pessimistic and gloomy considering the legacy that the author himself left in the annals of history.

Solomon was reportedly the richest and wisest man that ever lived second in wisdom only to the Messiah, Jesus whom he preceded. Solomon didn't only have favor with God but he also had favor with men. Kings and other rulers from throughout the East abundantly blessed him with presents of land, riches and precious commodities. He had enough to get whatever he wanted much less needed. But still he was led to coin the inquiry, "What profit hath a man of all his labor which he taketh under the sun?" (Ecclesiastes 1:3). In other words, what advantage, what benefit does a man get from his work here on earth? One would think that since we spend a portion of our lives preparing for work, another portion actually doing work and then the latter portion recovering from the result of work that there would be some key to abundant life in the work. If we look around us at the ceaseless cycle of generations, the question still remains. What do I gain if I am born today, die tomorrow and am soon forgotten? What is the profit in it? Why am I alive if sooner or later I am going to die and be soon forgotten? Ironically that is the mindset that many of us have been dealing with from generation to generation. The moment the naiveté of childhood, adolescents and teenage dependence on parents rubs off we are birthed into adulthood with a resolute ignorance of why we really exist.

Science, mans attempt to explain nature while explaining away God has miserably failed at shoring up the minds and consciences of a mentally, and psychologically apathetic human psyche. God has been shoved to the interior cubes or more recently dome-shaped church buildings on Sunday mornings throughout the United States and much of the Christian west. God, the central theme of the idea of life has been shelved for theories of evolution, the principles of random mutation, the idea of survival of the fittest and the belief in existentialism. We are taught five days a week that what we were taught in Sunday school or the Sunday morning sermon was just the bewitched ranting of a brainwashed Homo-sapien whose evolutionary progress physically does not equate to his mental digression. We are told that all those "stories" we read about in the bible are just that stories that actually are more in the realm of myth, fantasy and fairy tale, than non-narrative and narrative recollection of truth. You are ridiculed as a deviant, with a tendency to diverge from what is considered normal behavior due to your beliefs. To have a Christian world-view today is to surmount to being a bumbling mentally deranged human being. To buy into the belief and conviction that a God (i.e. Jesus Christ), is the one who controls the innumerable amounts of involuntary human mechanisms that allow us to live is to be dead to reality. However, to believe that we came to be, that we exist just because of a random shift in the cosmos. That this shift due to an abundance of entropic activity led to a big bang, and the natural creation of an organic soup from which all the elemental material for which all life forms emerged, is considered to be forward thinking.

That is essentially what we are fed almost daily in this secular driven world system. But God is the lifter of our heads. He desires to lift us from the trash heap of man's misconstrued knowledge of the universe, and to elevate us above even that which man could even comprehend. How could such a flawed creature as I, be expected to have dominion and put all these other beasts under subjection? How does God expect me to rule and set the standard and basically set the pace when I am not sure what pace really is or what the rules really are? But God says he is our encourager. He says that he does not expect us to do it on our own but rather that we should be doing it through Him. The Bible says that in him we live, move and have our being. And if we live, move and have our being in Him, and He is high and lifted up, that means that my head must also be lifted up. God gives us a treasure of counsel and advice on how to live life abundantly but we have allowed the problems of our life birthed in the fall of man to overwhelm the posture of promise that we had when we first heard the Word.

Therefore we ought to give more earnest heed to the things which we have heard, lest at any time we should let them slip.

Hebrews 2:1

What are the things that cause you to have a bent head? What are the issues of your life that at times causes you to doubt what God has already said? Is it the "you" that no one else knows? Who are you in the dark? How do you feel about who you are and about what others say that you are? Sometimes these are the things that keep us bowed down and depressed. We seldom take time out of our pursuit of life to actually assess our lives. Is life passing you by even though you are running full steam ahead? Slow down and look at your life and see if you are allowing God to make an impact or an impression on your lives. There is a difference between God making an impact and Him making an impression. One transforms your life eternally and the other causes a temporal change or elicits a moment of contemplation. God should be impacting your life not just making an impression on your lives. Worldly mentors, role models, people that we look to for advice or we admire for their achievements are the ones that we should expect or even look to, as ones to make an impression on our lives. Our savior Jesus Christ is our perfect example and His life, His mercy, His Spirit and the things of God are the factors that should be impacting our lives.

Think of the idea of a head lifted up. I am sure that you have lifted the head of a young child before or even the head of someone that you loved or just simply the head of friend. To lift a head is to direct someone's gaze from the floor to the sky. I remember raising my daughter's head when she had one of her moments of crying and I remember that it was almost like the sad feature of her face could not handle the lifting. When I lifted her head the tears ran down the side of her cheeks and her face immediately transformed from a sulk to a grin. The touching and the raising of her chin, directing her eyes into my eyes was all that she needed to gather relief from whatever it was that had been troubling her. If your life is overwhelmed with trouble recognize that there is one that has the power to lift your chin above it. He desires to take your eyes off the situation, and to put them into his presence.

How many of you can remember all the failures you had as a child? The way you answer that question depends on the degree to which you lived your early life. If you remembered most of the failures most likely your life as a child was starved of the experience of joy. If you remembered a few failures most likely your early life was a mixture of joy and some pain. And if you don't remember any of the failures most likely your life as a child was one of complete joy and merriment. There is no right or wrong answer to the question of remembered experience of failure because as each of us is different in appearance so too each of us is different in our experiences. The fact that some people remember these failures and some others don't points to the way in which God has wired us to be resilient. You can forget them if you wanted to, but some of us still choose to hold on to these events and happenings because they serve to somehow remind us of what it felt like so that we might be ready when the time comes to feel like that again.

Comfortability, that is the cry of mankind, and that is exactly the force against which nature and essentially God is fighting us to get out of. Paul said in his epistle to the Philippians that he had grown to be content in whatsoever state he found himself. We take that content to be comfortable, but the two are quite different in meaning, he was content—able to deal or tolerate his temporal situation but he was not comfortable, he was not resting in that position. The fact that God can work, regardless of our unique experiences, to give us an equal measure of peace and joy in the totality of our lives speaks of his powerful ability to lift our heads. But we must allow him to lift it. Someone resolved not to recover from a breakup, a damaged relationship, a financial loss, a medical setback, a business failure or even just from a mental breakdown due to stress, would be a difficult candidate to experience the blessing of a lifted head.

3.

What's in your Bag?

And David put his hand in his bag, and took thence a stone, and slang it, and smote the Philistine in his forehead, that the stone sunk into his forehead; and he fell upon his face to the earth.
1 Samuel 17:49

Isn't it strange that
princes and kings,
and clowns that caper
in sawdust rings, and
common people like you
and me
All have one thing in common?

Each of us is given a bag of
tools, a shapeless mass,
a book of rules.
And each of us must make
either stumblingblocks or
stepping stones.

R.L. Sharpe

    This poem brings amazing enlightenment to a key principle of life, the choices we make given the things that we have at our disposal determines the level of difficulty our lives walk will possess. What do you have in your bag? David carried five smooth stones, and with those stones he was on a mission to literally destroy the giant that had made its way into his life and the life of those around him. What are the things that you are carrying in your bag? How are you using the contents of your bag to exact survival in this sometimes, fierce world? Are the stones in your bag weapons, tools or building materials? The worth that your

28

life accumulates can be traced to the ways in which you spend the greatest commodity of your life—time.

Every man regardless of his station, rich or poor, star or unknown, hero or fan, all has this bag that they carry. Our bags may either be packed with smooth stones or rough rocks. Where do these stones or these rocks come from? How do they get into our bags? The way that we deal with the experiences of this life, the method that we use to bank the life changing events of our lives, all can be explanations for what and how these things get into our bags. It's not how these stones get into our bag or where they came from that is really of importance but it is how we use them that matter to God. He expects us to use these things to make something of our lives or rather to allow Him to make something of us through these stones. The Bible says that...ye are God's building. Jesus Christ is the wise master builder according to the book of 1 Corinthians 3:10. Our Lord and Savior Jesus Christ builds the foundation, and another builds upon it.

But let every man take heed how he buildeth thereupon.
1 Corinthians 3:10

What are you in the scheme of Christ's building project? Are you a bridge builder, or are you an erector of roadblocks? Are you constructing artful ways to overcome or are you just making ugly obstacles that bar even you from getting to the other side of your destiny? It's up to us; given the decisions that we make in our lives to take these issues that we face good or bad and turn them to our advantage.

I am not asking you to take an unrealistic optimistic view of things and not to recognize moments of pain and anguish and sorrow. However, I would expect you to have times of grief and sorrow as crisis is a natural part of life but you must use even the tragedy that you have faced and let it strengthen your resolve. Let it strengthen you to be a champion to prevent such tragedy in your life again, or in the lives of those with whom you come in contact. Careless handling of problems, issues and unfortunate circumstances in our lives is the culprit that must be blamed for much of the compounding of blockades and roadblocks in our lives.

Fear of failure, fear of rejection and fear of the fight are all the different obstacles that cause us to be moving in circles, always active but making no progress. The worth of our lives is also tied into the steps that we take to success, but if we are taking steps into the footprints that we already made are we really progressing? No, in fact we are just revisiting familiar territory, we aren't lost but we also aren't finding our way.

Problems and promises how is your bag stacked with them? Is it unevenly stacked with problems that unfairly place an undesirable burden on your shoulders? Or is it stacked with a good portion of promises that eases your burden?

Come unto me all ye that labor and are heavy laden, and I will give you rest. For my yoke is easy, and my burden is light.
Matthew 11:28,30

Jesus gives us a great promise in this statement found in the gospel of Matthew. He says that if we take on his yoke and his burden we will take on something easy and light. Jesus is setting forth a promise that if we immerse ourselves in Him we will experience the easing of our burdens because we would actually be taking on his burdens. Again we would be substituting the lack of worth in our life's issues by taking on the abundant worth of His life issues. Problems and promises will always coexist in our lives. The exchange or the balance, the ability to deal with the problems and continue to strive toward the promises is the only way that we can hope to live abundantly.

Aldous Huxley once said, "Every man who knows how to read has it in his power to magnify himself, to multiply the ways in which he exists, to make his life full, significant and interesting." Mr. Huxley made a very clear distinction in this statement by saying that the reader possesses the power to positively affect their lives. But many of us can attest to the fact that possession of power does not guarantee or immediately equal utilization of that power. I believe that in the spiritual primarily in the Christian context every Christian who has a mind steeped in praise has the power to magnify him or herself, to multiply the ways in which they live, to make their life abundant, important and worthwhile. But again having a Christian mindset without a Christian faith walk is like being an object at rest on the edge of a cliff. It possesses great potential energy-latent energy stored in its frame-but due to its immobility the power or energy is of no effect. Our aim should be to make God's power manifest through and in our lives.

Francis Bacon also said that knowledge is power. But in Christ it is the knowledge of God that gives power and not just any knowledge. It is with the mind that we praise God. Our mind is in control of our praise.

Be ye transformed by the renewing of the mind
Romans 12:2

It is also with the mind that we garner wisdom through the accumulation of knowledge, and the sorting out of the specifics from the non-specifics, and the essentials from the non-essentials of life.

The bags that we carry are a mix-match of distractions and destiny. Our lives should be a crusade in the classifying and sorting out of the things that are distractions from the things that are destiny. What has God placed in my path to direct me to my destined place versus what the devil has thrown in my path to create distraction. The questions that should come to mind daily should include—"Is this relationship God ordained or devil orchestrated? Should I really take that advice, it sounds good but can it actually be too good to be the truth? How will what God really has planned for me be affected? Will this lead to delay or a dead-end; or to deliverance and destiny in God's determined time? What are the pros and cons attached to my acceptance of this new standard into my life? How do we juggle the contents of our bags so that life is less than a burden?

Think of the last time that you had a carry a cumbersome bag home from the grocery. It could be either the walk from the store to the car, or from the car into the house. This heavy, often times absurdly packed bag can be a strain. It digs into the creases of the flesh in your hands, the skin of your palms are raw and red and irritated as blood rushes to the area. You are driven to switch from hand-to-hand several times in an effort to transport these goods safely (without dropping them) to your cupboard and your refrigerator. What is the problem? An over-packed, tedious load that could have been eliminated had the grocery store packer thought to distribute, sort or categorize the goods more appropriately. We walk through life switching from left to right in our belief systems, from fad to fad, not standing long enough for anything to really make it count for something substantial. And essentially we end up tossed and driven by every wind of doctrine. We are left with bruised egos, seared conscience and a disregard for morals because of the impression that the loads of distractions have brought to your life.

Jesus implores us to take his yoke and his burden. He said that his yoke is easy and his burden is light. The doctrine of an easy Christian life absent of any burden is false doctrine. This is due to the contemporary redefining of the word "burden" and even the word, "yoke". Burdens and yokes today connote bondage, wearisome task, and heaviness but in actuality a burden is just an added weight to carry. A yoke is just a standard of conduct. A feather, as light as it is, represents a burden. It is still an added weight to carry. A code of moral conduct, a more by which one directs business, social interaction and personal relations that is a yoke and a guide. God didn't only suggests exchanging our humanly burdens for his spiritual burden but he also desires us to help each other to bear our loads.

The apostle Paul urged the saints in Galatians 5 to bear ye one another's burdens and so fulfill the law of Christ. In this postulation we can see that Christ works in one of two ways to affect the severity of the burdens that we bear. He may directly relieve us of our burdens or He may work directly through the relationships that we have with others, in Christ, to bring us relief.

4.

The King In You

But ye are a chosen generation, a royals priesthood, an holy nation, a peculiar people; that ye should shew forth the praises of him who hath called you out of darkness into his marvelous light.
1 Peter 2:9

You are worthy enough to be called royalty. Royalty, it has a nice ring to it. The sounds of pomp and circumstance ring through my mind. However, reality soon hits and I am forced to assess my current circumstance. According to my understanding of royalty, my underrated standard of living does not equate to that entitlement. My access to the "things" that designate royalty must be much greater than it is right now. The fringe benefits of the title of royalty should far outweigh what I currently experience. That is the predicament that many of us find ourselves in; saved, and wanting to believe that we are royalty as the Bible says. However, we are hindered by self-doubt birthed in our own analysis of the struggles we face on the rubric of worldly standards.

Being counted as a royal priesthood is one of the basic fundamental and foundational truths on which our salvation and justification stands. This truth however can many times be the stumbling block to our spiritual development. The inability to wrap our physical minds around the spiritual truth of attained royalty through Christ is what keeps many of us missing the abundance that God has for us.

What does it truly mean to have a king inside of you? This is to know that somewhere in your mortal flesh dwells a spirit that is so powerful it contains in it a majesty and sovereignty unlike no other. This is a king that the rest of the world is anxiously awaiting to take His rightful place of

authority. The world awaits our coronation, our crowning.
When kings and queens still ruled this world, the period of
time leading up to the coronation of a successor to the
throne was always either a time of celebration, anticipation
or even anxiety. An ailing or deceased monarchy many times
marked a period of political and civil unrest. The simple
announcement of a successor to the throne was heralded as
a joyous occasion.

Coming to our royal potential begins with having a
kingly mindset. How do we get a kingly mindset? It is
similar to attaining a mind for success. Business gurus
always say that the key to success in industry and financial
investment is to develop a success mentality. If I believe that
I am success in my mind eventually my heart will be inspired
to come to terms with what my mind chooses to focus on.
Royal potential is first evident in what I would like to call the
"majestic swagger". Many misinterpret kingdom
mindedness, and the exhibition of royal potential through an
elevated thought life, as a mark of haughtiness, and pride.
We must however, remember that haughtiness and pride are
rooted in false pretense. Developing a kingdom mindset and
already possessing the accouterments of royalty are different
from being of peasant status and posing as royalty. The act
of calling our minds to the awareness of our true status is all
part of the equipping or grooming that is necessary for one to
be properly prepared for kingdom outcomes in our lives.

True royalty doesn't have to be reminded on a daily
basis that they are royalty. They just have to be aware of the
distinguishing features of their lives. The attention, the
privilege, the favor shown toward them is all that is
necessary to plant a seed that confirms royal status. Prince
Charles and Prince Edward of England from quite young
were directly and indirectly predisposed to their status of
royalty. Acclimation to such a distinct position in life is
unavoidable even if measures are taken to create a shroud of
discretion in the personal lives of royalty. Royalty is a
birthright that is as much part of oneself as ones name.

Prince Charles, as a young boy, was not operating in any ruling capacity but still was and is considered royalty. It doesn't begin with an appointment to a position it is something one is usually born into. From birth one is then groomed to properly execute the duties of the office of kingship.

> **Thou shalt also be a crown of glory in the hand of the Lord, and a royal diadem in the hand of thy Lord.**
> **Isaiah 62:3**

The way we think about royalty has to be the first change to take place, in order for us to really crown the king in us. Latent power is both an asset and a deficit depending on how it is utilized or under-utilized. A king's title, power and influence is at its greatest potential to affect change at the moment that king is elevated and recognized publicly as a king. This takes place at his crowning or coronation.

All of us that name the name Jesus and count ourselves as saved and sanctified Christians can understand that the experience of freedom in Christ is instantaneous and is as momentous as the statements leaving our lips agreeing with the change in our hearts toward Christ, and His godhead. However, we forfeit any other benefits beyond freedom in Christ when we never mature to the level of mentally seeing ourselves as kings and queens through Him. We walk around as crown princes and princesses, living with just enough when God promised more than enough. Are you just an heir apparent to a promised throne wasting your promise away ignorant of your status or just wrapped in false pride?

The Bible says in the gospel of Luke that Jesus promised the disciples an endowment of power from on high. Imagine that the disciples has waited for the power as God promised, received that power and then relished in the knowledge that they had this power but never went out and proclaimed the Gospel, healed the sick or neglected the experience of suffering and persecution for His name sake. The power that they would then possess would have been one attached to vainglory. In other words, having the power and not using it is just as good as not having it at all. Possessing a remedy, a solution or a cure to a major ailment that the world is facing but choosing to keep it a secret is not too far and separated from not really having any answer. Remedies, solutions and cures are only important if they are used. When we take the steps to be crowned we are really recognizing where the power lies. The power of a monarch is symbolically embodied in their crown, in the head. The king in us is waiting for his crown to be rightly placed.

> **And the men of Judah came, and there they anointed David king over the house of Judah.**
> **2 Samuel 2:4**

Our next step in fulfilling the king in us is to live like royalty. In order for us to live like royalty we have to fully understand what a royal lifestyle entails. Royalty appears both in the Old and New Testaments. The Hebrew word for royalty is derived from the root word, "malkuyah" which literally can be translated rule, dominion, empire, kingdom, realm or reign. To live, as royalty then in the Old Testament sense is to accept that one has a kingdom, or dominion over which we have rights over which to rule. Royalty, as used in the New Testament, comes from the Greek root word, "basilekos" which literally means a foundation of power, or sovereignty. In the Old Testament royalty was assigned to those who possessed, while in the New Testament it was used to describe those who were built on a base of power. Therefore, royalty is both a term that describes origin (foundation) and possession (wealth).

Royalty lives with an understanding that they have special privileges to which others don't have access. Royalty depends on favor and not on credit history. When it comes to royalty credit is derived not from savings and expenditures but rather from ones name.

> **...fill thine horn with oil, and go, I will send thee to Jesse the Bethlehemite: for I have provided me a king among his sons.**
>
> **1 Samuel 16:1**

Jesse, the Bethlehemite, a farmer of humble background, father of eight with a modest wealth of sheep, was chosen to be the father of the next king of Israel. Jesse was the father of King David. When David was at home with his father he wasn't David the King, but rather he was David, the shepherd. But yet still we can see from the aforementioned scripture text in the first book of Samuel that the Lord considered David king even before the prophet Samuel officially anointed him. One of the greatest examples of the principle of crowning the king inside of us, in order for the greatest potential in us to shine forth, was the story of a shepherd boy turned king, David. If there is any illustration in the Bible that gives insight into the worth that we have in the eyes of God it is in the example of David. David stood as a notable character in scripture not only for his body of writing in the poetic psalms but also for his story. The ordinariness of his character coupled with the extraordinary achievements of his life speaks volumes of where God looks for worth in someone. Why did God choose the least of the sons, of a poor unknown farmer, in the lowliest of regions in Judah? It was because God was showing us what He values. He was showing us that He could birth greatness even in the lowliest of places. God does not depend on location, status or position to assign greatness. Rather he looks for availability.

> **But the Lord said unto Samuel, Look not on his countenance, or on the height of his stature; ...for the Lord seeth not as man seeth; for man looketh on the outward appearance, but the Lord looketh on the heart.**

1 Samuel 16:7

It was not in David's outward appearance, or even David's righteous actions that God found him to be a man after His own heart, it was in David's ability to see the fragility in his person, and recognize where his true power came from. David constantly returned to the feet of God fully open, repentant and boldly coming before the Father hiding nothing of his faults. This never took away from David's appointment to royalty. He was still anointed king of Judah first and then Israel proper. His journey from anointing to appointing was one of struggle, rejection and threats on his life by the one who held the current appointment but David yet and still was king to be. The Spirit of the Lord was with him and the Spirit of the lord as promised by Jesus Christ is in us once we are filled, once we receive, once we present our bodies as a living sacrifice and once we accept the promise. God counted you worthy enough to surpass even what He did for David. Therefore crown the king in you and experience the abundance that is due to royalty as yourself.

5.

A Friend of God:
Positioned for Perfection

**And the Lord said, Shall I hide from Abraham that
thing which I do;....
For I know him, that he will command his children
and his household after him, and they shall keep
the way of the Lord, to do justice and judgment;
Genesis 18:17, 19**

Oh what a friend we have in Jesus, all thy sins and
grief's to bear. What a privilege to carry, everything to God
in prayer. These are the opening lines to a powerful hymn
that I remember singing when I was a young boy growing up
in church. Every time I heard those lyrics sung it struck me
that Jesus, who I understood to be a mighty God, could
possibly condescend enough to be my friend. My friends as I
understood it to be were those who I could play with. They
were those who I could trust with my secrets and those who
I could speak plainly with. I didn't have to pretend with my
friends. If something hurt me, I knew that I could express
my feelings of hurt with my friend and it would be just fine.
Friends were boys or girls with whom I was close and
comfortable. A friend could occupy my private space and I
wouldn't be offended or uneasy. So, how could this great big
God become a friend of mine? Could it be true that this God
of ours counts us worthy enough to be our friend?

Some of us can count the number of friends that we
have on one hand. While others cannot count the number of
friends that they have. Our mere psychological makeup
predisposes us to desire friendship and close
companionship. The Bible says that Jesus is more than a
friend, to those who are called by His name. But how many
of us can really say that we have a relationship with Christ
that would even approach friendship?

40

As we examine the idea of friendship with our Lord and savior, Jesus Christ, one must look at the blueprint or the model of friendship as recorded in the experiences that scripture give us concerning this type of relationship. One of the first examples of a godly friendship both in nature and actual substance was the relationship forged between God and Abraham. Abraham was a friend of God. What was it about Abraham that set him apart as a man to whom God sought to develop a friendship? Was it something about Abraham's personality or character that delineated him from the other men that lived around his time?

We first hear of Abraham in Genesis 11:26 where he is listed by his former name, Abram, as part of the genealogy of Shem, one of the sons of Noah. It is almost insignificant the way that God gives instruction to Abraham to leave the country of his birth. God instructs him not only to leave his homeland but also to leave his father's house and to go to a land yet to be revealed. This almost seemingly minor divine directive actually is the beginning of the scriptural record of God creating a nation, separated onto Him. The question still stands why Abraham? From examination of all related text the answer to this question must lie in the essence of God's favor. Abraham was chosen simply because God designed it that way. The choosing of Abraham and the direction that God gave him heralded the beginning of the dispensation of promise. The manner in which God was dealing with mankind and the way in which man was able to approach God was also changing. Promises were made to Abraham and his descendants and as long as they held up their side of the resulting covenant these promises would be made manifest in their lives.

Friendship, unlike what some people consider love, is not at first sight. It has to be developed over time. You may see someone's potential to be your friend at your first meeting but that is just it potential. It does not become a friendship until you have been through something and that person has showed themselves trustworthy and accountable to you in some way, shape or form before you consider them a friend. Friendship in a relationship depends a great deal on the levels of intimacy in that union. Love at its basis level does not have to include any intimacy or close contact. We can love each other from quite a distance. We can develop a degree of love for something or someone without ever actually having any intimate time with them. However, friendship in its purest sense takes a level of intimacy over a period of time. The decided period of time is solely at the discretion of the people involved. However, nevertheless there must a time of close contact, of communication, and of exchange of feelings.

When was it that the relationship between Abraham and God became a friendship? Was it at the initial call for him to leave Haran or was it a relationship that was developed over time due to Abraham's interact, reaction and adherence to the direction that God had given him? The bible says that Abraham departed as the Lord had spoken unto him to do. This shows that he was obedient in character from the outset. But then the moment it gets a bit tough in the place that God had directed him to go, Abraham resorts to go down to Egypt. This was the first test of Abraham's worthiness in the eyes of God.

As we develop in our own relationship with our Lord and Savior we too will be tested. These aren't test to urge failure but rather they are test that serve to discipline. Any test that God puts us through is not to merely throw a setback in our way but rather to set us up for the greater diversions that life will hand to us. Abraham pretty much succumbed to the fear of the ensuing famine. I believe that if he had stayed in Canaan and called upon God to spare him and sustain his family in the midst of the famine, God would have done it. However, Abraham didn't and chose to pursue the comfort of Egypt.

He did like us. We choose to pursue the comfort of our Egypt, the world. God sometimes puts testing situations in our life, financial lack, social obstacles and educational delays. We look upon these situations as setbacks. We see them as strategies by the enemy to keep us down. It is true that the enemy does use the opportunity of Godly testing to plant seeds of discouragement in our minds. This leads to us losing sight of the lesson that God is teaching in the loss. We fail to see God's desire to show us that our financial state should not be the God that anchors our emotional state of mind. He wants us to see that societal acceptance should be of a lower priority in our lives to godly acceptance. He wants us to know that knowing Him and understanding what we are in Him outweighs any academic achievement or accolades that one could attain to.

Despite Abraham's choice to go to Egypt, God does not cancel him out as a man of little faith, in fact God stands back and allows him to witness the power of divine favor on his life even in a circumstance that may have appeared life threatening. It was favor that led to God's choice of Abraham and it was favor that led to him deceiving the king of Egypt (Pharaoh) with regard to his wife, and escaping unharmed. In fact, he didn't have to escape he left freely at the behest of Pharaoh. Pharaoh's men escorted him out with his wife and all that he owned just because of the favor of God on his life and on how that favor toward him equaled a curse toward anyone in opposition or contradiction to him.

And I will bless them that bless thee, and curse him that curse thee;
Genesis 12:3

As I think of this first test and the exchange between Pharaoh and Abraham and the idea of a developing friendship between God and Abraham, the next concept that comes to mind is when does a friendship become a friendship? Also the question of who initiates a friendship? In other words, does a friendship have to be initiated in two directions? Does a friendship have to be pursued by both parties for it to culminate in true friendship? Is God the one pressing for friendship in this circumstance or is it Abraham?

I do not desire to postulate a character upon God of being a Lord that needs to seek friends, because He puts these parameters and pre-assessments on the life of Abraham to read his response. I believe that in this respect both Abraham and God were moving in the direction of friendship. Think about it, God starts the test, Abraham chooses other than God would have initially desired him to choose, but God does not give up on him. God still afflicts Pharaoh and his family on behalf of Abraham. God looks out for him. Why? It is because God was interested in developing a friendship, and He had keen insight into the character of Abraham. God knew that Abraham was a worshipper.

The English word worship comes from the Old English word "worthship" it is a word that denotes the worthiness of the one receiving the special honor or devotion. Abraham identified the worthiness of God even before the promise of God was made manifest in his life. Remember how we first heard of Abraham, God shows up, and says, leave your homeland, your father's house, and take your house and your property and travel to this land that I will show you. Abraham leaves without question. God promises him a personal and a generational blessing yet to come. He traveled to Canaan in total obedience to God with very little direction, and upon arrival in this land that is already occupied receives another proclamation. The Lord appears to him again and repeats a pronouncement of blessing:

Unto thy seed will I give this land;
Genesis 12:7

The key term that I want to focus on is the clause "I will give..."Will is an auxiliary verb that is used to indicate simple future time. It is used to express a determination, an obligation. "Will" is used to express an expectation. When God says I will give this land to thy seed He is saying sometime in the future this land that you stand in right now is going to be yours and your seed. God didn't say this land is yours now, He said it will be yours. Abraham did not yet possess the promise; he was getting a glimpse of it. He was not yet grasping it, but he had the wherewithal to worship God anyway. Abraham was a worshipper.

He travels to Egypt to escape the famine in Canaan and deceives the Pharaoh believing that it was the only way he could protect himself and his family. Abraham in a moment of struggle almost wholly forgets the promise of God made to him. Some may argue that this stems from Abraham's lack of knowledge of who God was. He may have placed God almighty in the same realm as the pagan idols and gods that he may have encountered in his early life. He knew of the promise that God made but he did not yet know of the power that God possessed to make the promise come to pass.

Say, I pray thee, thou art my sister: that it may be well with me for thy sake; and my soul shall live because of thee.
Genesis 12:13

Abraham in this scripture text is expressing his doubt in the Divine and his dependence on his own flesh. Abraham was depending on his ability to connive to, as he saw it, forego any harm that may have come to him. Ultimately God shows him favor and vindicates him and allows him safe passage out of the clutches of the enemy. Through the entire ordeal that he witnessed in Egypt, Abraham gets a glimpse of the power that this covenanted God has through His affliction of the Egyptians. And when he returns to Canaan, Abraham does what he knows best, he worships God. He returns to the land and to the altar that he had erected to God, and there he called on the name of the Lord.

We see that the first principle or character trait that delineates friends of God are the fact that friends of God must be worshippers of God. How do I know that I am a worshipper? Or how do I become a worshipper? What was it that made Abraham a worshipper? Was it a deep down sentiment, or a genetic character trait? In fact, I believe it was neither of these but rather it was a practice that Abraham developed over time.

Abraham's worship was a spiritual practice of reverent devotion and an allegiance pledged to God. His worship was evidenced by the ritual of erecting an altar to God and calling on the name of God, and offering sacrifice on the altar to God. His worship was manifested in the physical steps he took in showing reverence but even deeper than that, were the spiritual steps that took place deep down in his soul, as he desired to approach the face of God in these rituals.

Abraham's worship was provoked by the promise that God placed on his life. His worshipful spirit eventually plays a major role in the resulting friendship that God has with him. When come to a saving knowledge of Jesus Christ, we too are made heirs to the promises that God made way back to the generations of Abraham. The spoken word of God's promise to Abraham, which has now become the written word of His scripture is a word spoken to you too, if you have accepted Him into your life.

6.

Price Paid

And he that reapeth receiveth wages, and gathereth fruit unto life eternal: that both he that soweth and he that reapeth may rejoice together.
John 4:36

George and Jenny walked into the car dealership. Their old car was on the fritz and they needed to replace it as soon as possible. They didn't have the money but they were bold enough to walk into the local automobile dealership. They believed that if they just walked around, examined, sat in and maybe even tried out a few of the cars on the lot they might find something that could replace their present vehicle that had become little more than a heap on wheels.

George had a plan in mind. He was going to walk around the lot and search for the cheapest thing on wheels. Anything was better than what he already had. Then he was going to construct the best argument he could to persuade the dealer to give him at his price.

Jenny had her own plan in mind. She was going to also examine the cars on the lot but she was intending that whatever they found they would trade in their vehicle and then depend on their credit to cover the remaining amount on the price of the car of their choice.

The middle-aged couple walked in together but went their separate ways. Jenny traveled in the direction of the luxury cars and SUVs and George traveled in the direction of the second-hand family vans and cars. They were two minds with one goal, to get a new car. One was intending to grovel and beg to get what he needed, and the other was planning to use a business strategy to get what she needed.

They stayed in the lot for about a good half-hour, trying locks, peering into trunks and bonnets, looking over engines and examining the dashboards of several vehicles. Then they came to a conclusion. They both had their fancies set on a mid-sized SUV, black in color, leather interior and fully automated. But there was a problem, George saw no way that they could get it at the time because it was out of what he perceived to be their price range. However, Jenny had a much different outlook she saw the potential that was in their old jalopy and she knew that they had decent credit.

George said, "It looks nice and I would love to have one of these fancy types of cars too but right now, I do not think that we could afford it." Jenny replied, "Do you like it? Because I like it!" George nodded his response but yet still in his mind there was doubt. He liked the car but he knew that his skills of coercion were not good enough to garner this type of a deal. They debated back and forth for some time over whether it was a wise thing to even pursue getting this new, eye-catching vehicle. Their exchange got animated at times but never lost control and in fact started to garner some attention from the sales clerks situated around the lot. Then a young sales woman came over and offered her input.

Jenny was delighted by the support that the sales lady was giving her in her selection and George was agitated thinking that the young sales woman was just trying to get a quick sale. Before long they were seated at the saleswoman's desk discussing the options. She asked about their old car. She asked about their income. She asked about the reasons for which they would be using the new vehicle. As the questions progressed, George got more and more depressed. In fact to him it all looked bleak.

Jenny on the other hand was getting more and more excited. The young sales woman asked to be excused so that she could speak further with the manager of sales concerning the needs of the couple. They agreed and as she left the office, the couple sat steering into space.

Jenny dreamed of driving the black SUV off the lot and George dreamed of continuing the search. After only ten minutes the sales woman returned and tells them that she thinks she could do something for them. She said that the dealership was willing to take their old car for a modest fee and would credit the remainder considering that their credit was in good shape. George was hesitant but Jenny was ready to get things done. Eventually they filled out the credit application, traded in their old car and were driving out of the lot with their new car. They came in as far as they knew it with no money, just a little hope and left with a new car.

Believe it or not, that is how many of us need to come into the knowledge of Christ. We need to come in broke, broken and with nothing but hope. The old car was the deposit they made and the bank paid the remainder. They owed the dealer nothing after that day. They only owed the bank that had already paid the price for the car. Our old issues, problems and messed up circumstances that we come to God with are our deposit, and the salvation covered new life that we get in return is the price paid in full. But understand this we don't owe God a salvation note but we do have to understand that our life is not our own. Eventually after paying the required amount of payments on the car loan, the car becomes our property. There is no such point we reach in Christ, he continues to give us upgrades and refurbishment for the life of his investment in us.

The price paid on our behalf is incalculable. The Bible says, "the wages of sin are death". However, we also understand that "the gift of God is eternal life through Christ Jesus." This statement of faith and belief is repeated probably thousands of times in the course of worship in any Christian home, congregation or heart. We believe that we have victory over death, the second death because Jesus Christ has condescended to pay the price that we could have never afforded to disperse to God's account. Regardless of the six figure incomes and greater, that men and women throughout this world have been able to accrue over the years, no man has been able to attach a qualitative figure to the value of human life. We may try to assess the gains and losses that one may experience because of the disconnect caused by a person being removed from our lives through the civil court system. Million dollar verdicts have been leveled against hospitals, doctors, insurance companies, corporate institutions, pharmaceutical firms and even other human beings accused in wrongful death suits. However, these large rewards of money never really repair the breach created by the death of that loved one.

It isn't so much the fact that the price is paid it is more that God counted you worthy enough to pay it. God did not have to send His son to die on our behalf. He chose to do so. Some believe that God had to do it or else. Or else what? Imagine God did not go the way of human redemption through the sacrificial work of Jesus Christ. Would human kind even have a chance? How would life be like for man today? We may never know because to conjecture on it would be to question the inerrant will of God. It was God's will that man would go through what he has gone through, and still is going through because God wanted man to make a conscience, self-directed decision to believe in Jesus Christ. Belief cannot be coerced and faith isn't faith unless it is self-attained.

For the law having a shadow of good things to come, and not the very image of the things, can never with those sacrifices which they offered year by year continually make the comers thereunto perfect.

Hebrews 10:1

Prior to the dispensation of grace, and before the arrival of Jesus Christ—the God man in the midst of His creation, man lived according to the law. The law referred to the counsel of God passed down to Moses on Mount Sinai during the ancient Hebrew people's sojourn in the wilderness. After the exodus from Egypt, after the people of God were freed from the clutches of the world system and were separated unto God in the wilderness, God set out to establish an order to the systematic lifestyle of his people.

Hence we have the establishment of the book of the law. The Law was to be the orderly system of rules and regulations by which the people of God were to govern their lives. The Law was to be a standard against which the people would measure the sanctity of their lives. It also served as a tool by which God could show the people what value He saw in human life. According to God's law all human life is counted as valuable. The fact that the Bible says that man was created in God's image is enough to show the value attached to our life. Everyone was equal in the eyes of God's law. Laws were established to set forth God's expectations for man's interaction and relationship with Him and with each other. Ceremonial rights and religious rituals were established so as to create an avenue by which the sinner could as it were recover from a bout of transgression. Sacrifice of bulls, goats and even doves, the typed dependent on ones economic standing served as recompense for a law broken or a sin performed by a member of the community of God. These sacrifices and the blood that was spilled in the process served as a symbolic covering of sin. However, as the scripture says in Hebrews chapter 10, it did not make the one offering the sacrifice perfect. It did not destroy the stain of the sin but rather worked as a mask to cover that sin in the eyes of God. The blood of that innocent animal, young and untouched hid the scar of the worshippers sin, but it did not do the complete work of remaking the sinner into one who was sinless.

Jesus Christ came into this world in the form of a man. He condescended to bless the womb of a virgin never before defiled by the seed of a mere mortal man. He encountered the assault of sin, the temptation and the physical ordeal of living as a human and then he gave his life as the perfect sacrifice. The Bible says:

But when the time had fully come, God sent forth his Son, born of a woman, born under the law, to redeem those who were under the law, so that we might receive adoptions as sons. And because you are sons, God has sent the Spirit of his Son into our hearts, crying 'Abba' Father!

Galatians 4:4-6

Jesus was born under the law to save us from the law and to bring us into God's grace through his perfect and all fulfilling sacrifice for our sin. Jesus became sin, but never sinned to save us from the penalty of our own sin. It is awesome just thinking about it. Imagine if we had to pay sacrificially for everything that we have ever done that was contrary to the law of God. The list of the people capable of gathering an adequate bounty of wealth by which they would make their sacrifice would be slim to none.

God saw us worthy enough to make the ultimate investment. All the wealth and riches that we accrue in this world and this life—monetarily stems from our ability or talent in a given area. Some of us possess wealth in our ability to speak and motivate others. Others of us possess wealth in our ability to construct and design with our hands. While others of us possess the ability to inspire others to say, to do or to think. These are all abilities that stem from the life that we have been blessed to live. These are all abilities that we are able to partake of because of life. If I have no life I cannot do any of these things.

We build wealth through giving of our lives in these different arenas. And this is exactly the same thing that Jesus Christ did on our behalf. He gave his life to gain the wealth of saved souls, whose transformed lives will ultimately stand as a testimony to his wondrous power, and as another opportunity for him to get the consequential glory.

What is the price of death? What is the price of the death of our Savior? Why was the necessary wage of sin death? Jesus had to die because the covenant had to be broken. The covenant of the law as it stood with the blood of goats and bulls covering the altar, the smoke of burning incense and sweet smelling spices was becoming a stink to the nostrils of God. The repetitive acts of sacrifice showed that man was revisiting sin rather than taking the steps of true repentance. He wasn't turning away from sin but rather was trying his best to walk around sin or face the same direction but just keep his eyes off of it. God needed to do an all-encompassing work. He needed to take away what was established in order to put into place what was to be.

We are daily bombarded with price tags. They adorn cars, clothes, books, food and even individuals. The simple process of making a purchase can easily remove the price tags that invade our lives. We give up something in order to get something. We give of our earnings to get the things that we need. We give financially in proportion to the listed price, and that is the only way that we could acquire the goods and services that we need. The give and take of buying and selling was definitely in effect when Jesus Christ *gave his life as a ransom for many.* We were bought. Our price was paid and Jesus' mission was complete.

7.
Possessing Perfect Love

And now abideth faith, hope, love, these three; but the greatest of these is love.
1 Corinthians 13:13

There was a story of a woman who was searching for love. All her life she had experienced what she considered unrequited love, tough love. Her parents hugged and kissed her as a child and told her she was a beautiful gift and they would always love her. They promised to love her but they failed in their promise. She had an older sister and an older brother who seemed to be getting more love than her. First her father left to go to war and he never returned, so his love was the first to go. Then it was her mother who began to be involved with another man and soon her love for her daughter waxed cold as she concentrated on the love of her new husband. Alas she was left with her brother and sister and they well were also seeking their own avenues of love and eventually the family broke up.

This young girl became a young woman and sought to get love from young men in the community. She wasn't of nobility or a high caste and everyone knew that her mother was on her second husband. This woman's reputation proceeded her and as a result she could only attract the wrong type of man. Not at all interested in love but rather just interested in getting physical with her. She heard the usual, you're beautiful, you're a gift even occasionally she heard in the midst of passion, "I love you!" She heard it so much in those situations that she thought the only way she could be loved was if she succumbed to the physical advances.

Remember she was searching for love. And unfortunately to suffice her need for the words, "I love you!" she ended up pursuing a life of prostitution. What could be better, the men said, "I love you!" and she also got paid and they stuck around as long as their money could last. She had found love.

And then one day a man came to town, that totally changed her understanding of what love was. And this man was of no real regard in appearance and he offered her no money, it wasn't his physical features or his finances but rather it was his words. He spoke so eloquently of love and gave her a new definition of love. He spoke of love unconditional, a love that surpassed all the sin that one could have indulged, a love that made one whole. He spoke of a love that this broken woman needed.

She had heard of how this man had healed a villager of evil spirits. He had even cast spirits out of another prostitute. He had raised a woman's son from his deathbed, cleansed a leper, and made a blind man see. This woman purposed it in her heart that she would meet this man.

She couldn't worry about the words of others, the jeers, or the nasty looks she needed to see Him and see Him soon. I t just happened that this man had a date to be at the house of one Simon the Pharisee. This woman gathered all that she had a sizable number of shekels and she went to the perfumery to buy a precious alabaster box of ointment. She would present this to the man, the man that had redefined love for her.

She entered that house Simon's house that night uninvited. She walked with her head down not wanting to face the looks, trying to tune out the voices but determined to meet the man. She had seen him from afar but when she entered the room it was as if she was drawn to the side of the room where he sat. And as if overwhelmed with this same love that He spoke of, she fell at his knees and did what only she knew to do. She washed his feet to show him pleasure. She was overwhelmed it was as if when she touched Him her brokenness was healed. She cried and with every tear mingled with the precious ointment she washed his feet. She had no towel and she used her hair to wipe his feet clean. Even at his feet she had found love. She had finally found love. And her sins were forgiven. Her search for love ended with her discovery of man who wanted her soul and her spirit and not just her physical body.

How great is your love? How much do you love the people in your life? How much do you love yourself? What is your definition of love? What kinds of love have you experienced first hand? What experience in your life can you put your finger on and say this is true love? Many of us would point to that first tingling feeling we felt when we saw that girl or boy that really struck our fancy some years ago. Again we might think of our first strong feelings of love as that time we first saw the birth of our son or daughter.

Regardless of the time, or the feeling that we attach to that sensation of love many of us never really are sure that it is love. Love has become to many, as a famous musician once said about peace, a fleeting illusion to be pursued but never attained.

As we grow in the Lord and in our understanding of our relationship to Him, it may start out being a fleeting or an escaping feeling but it should not remain that way. Maturing in Christ is synonymous with realizing what the Lord considers love to be. Your idea of love and your understanding of what love is should begin with God. Your love for God should be at such a level that regardless of what happens to you, it remains solid and real. Your love for God should be the first place that you determine to make love more than just an illusion and make it a reality. Only then can love as you know it, and as you practice it on those in your life become real.

How many of you know that God allows everything that happens to you? There are times when what is happening to us, what is happening in us, what is happening for us and what we are going through leads us to question the love of God. But you have to understand that God loves you in spite of what you put Him through. He loves you and there is nothing that you can do about it.

What dimension is your love? In 1 Corinthians 13, the apostle Paul gives us what could possibly be considered the greatest dissertation on the virtues of love. Love is a term that is thrown around in this day and age, and is used to describe anything from as minor as admiration, attraction and care for someone to feelings as deep as lust, obsession and strong affection. The looseness with which love is approached can be blamed on the loose definition that is given for love.

What exactly is love? The New American Webster Dictionary defines love as—*any* strong liking or affection. The problem with this definition is the use of the word *any* suggesting that *whatever* constitutes love. There are too many people that have the idea that love is whatever you feel that it is. These people have a far greater grasp of what love is not, than what love is. Think of it. He says I love you but he still lies and cheats. He says I love you but he can't wait for marriage. He says I love you but he still treats you like a second-class citizen. He says I love you but he can be so selfish. He says I love you but he leaves the moment it gets difficult. These are all examples of experiences that some of us have faced in the name of love. Love as we know it is easy, but love as God wants it takes work.

Our understanding of love comes from our own personal experience of love and most times we seek love in the form in which we acquired it. In the story the woman's understanding of love was based on how she experienced love and therefore that was why she sought those words, "I love you!" in the way she did. But aren't you glad that God counts you worthy enough, just as He counted her worthy enough, to experience perfect love from Him.

This woman had to redefine her dimension of love. What dimension is your love? It takes overcoming personal prejudice, self-fulfillment, me-centric thinking, fleshly urges and the belief that life should be a cakewalk. Love is a two-sided sport and not a one-sided game. Many of us are playing games with ourselves, dealing the cards and playing each hand in turn. It's not a sport in the sense that is a mere diversion but that it is an event that takes the participation of both sides.

The final verse in 1 Corinthians 13 says, "And now abideth faith, hope, love, these three; but the greatest of these is love." The greatest of these is love. Why is love the greatest? What about faith? The Bible says without faith it is impossible to please God. How can love surpass faith in greatness? This scripture text suggests that there is a graduated value or stepping system involved in our attainment of the spirit of love. To have a spirit of love is counted as the greatest thing. Does this mean that love replaces faith? In fact I believe that it means that in order for us to know what love really is we must first begin with faith.

It all starts with faith. Hebrews 11:1 says: "Now faith is the substance of things hoped for..." This means that faith is substantive. It is the tangible intangible. It gives (proof) or witness to things that are invisible to the naked natural eye. That statement alone shows the power that is possessed in faith. Faith is powerful and gets its power from its even more powerful source—God. The bible says that faith comes by hearing and hearing comes by the Word of God. This faith in turn gives us hope in the promises that the Word of God makes to us. Hebrews 11:3 says that through faith we understand that the worlds were framed by the Word of God, so that things which are seen were not made of things which do appear. This means that God's word is able to create something from nothing. Faith believes in something while seeing nothing. It is believing first and then seeing after.

We know that faith comes by hearing but how does faith stay and in staying how does it birth in us hope that grows into love of Jesus Christ. The Gospel of Jesus Christ (the Word) deposits faith in us. Faith gives us hope. It creates substance for our hope. Faith in Christ creates in us hope. The hope that we have in Christ's promise develops a love in us for God, for self and eventually for others. Hope works in us a love.

What are the dimensions of love? As there are dimensions with matter in the natural, when we speak of the spiritual there are also dimensions. In the same way that solid matter has dimensions, so too does our love possess dimensions to it. Love can be one-dimensional. One-dimensional love is only concerned with either the length or the width of my own feelings. Is love for you getting what *you* need? Is love for you satisfying *your* pleasure? Or is it building *yourself* up while tearing others down? Notice the central subject in each of the above descriptions of love-- you, your and yourself. One-dimensional love is me-centric love that is consumed with fulfilling selfish needs of affection, attention and care.

Two-dimensional love is a love concerned for others only on a level plane. This is the type of love that helps others only to advance your own good. Two-dimensional love is a love of that is filled with conditions. It appears to be genuine love and may even include life-giving sacrifices. However, what this love has in appearance is much less than what it possesses in motives. This love may include life-giving sacrifice but not life-sacrificing giving. In two-dimensional love you just give of *your* life to get *your* fill of love. This is the type of love that meets the needs of others simply to get the credit. Two-dimensional love is the kind that appears brotherly and sisterly and caring but that is actually all that it is, an appearance.

We are spirit beings that live in a physical body. We are three-dimensional having spirit, body and soul. One might think that a three-dimensional scope of love would fulfill our needs as human beings. But we have to remember that we are aspiring not for love that is ideal for us but love that is perfect in the eyes of God. Three-dimensional love is concerned only for those who you feel are of your same status. Those who you know can return on a good favor. This is a love that is birthed in, focused on and stationed in the satisfaction of whatever our physical body's says is good and pleasing. The woman in the story that opened this chapter believe it or not, she wasn't just one-dimensional, or just two-dimensional, she was three-dimensional even in her mess. She was fulfilled mentally, emotionally, and physically but that wasn't enough. And for us three-dimensional isn't enough. If love for you is the fulfillment of mind and what you can perceive with your senses you are not experiencing the God type of love for you. If love for you is the fulfillment of bodily urges and the fulfillment of emotions as you connect with a soul mate this still is not enough, God desires even more.

There is a fourth dimension of love. A dimension that is borne out in the love that God shows toward us. A dimension that supersedes and exceeds all expectations, conditions or the personal cares that comes with love in the other dimensions. Love as we know it today is derived from 4 Greek terms that actually describe love in its many facets. And often times we define love or acquire love according to one given dimension or a combination of dimensions but we seldom get the complete and perfect love shown toward us by others that God has to offer.

In the first epistle of John and the fourth chapter and eighteenth verse it says there is no fear in love, but perfect love casteth out fear. If we dwell in this dimension of love we cannot sin or be hindered by sin, and this love fulfills all needs. The Bible tells us that as believers in Jesus Christ we must reflect the image of Christ. Jesus Christ is the metaphorical Sun and we represent the moon. The moon shines because it reflects the light of the Sun.

God counted us as worthy enough to act as reflectors for Him in a dark and dying world. As reflectors we are the first receivers of the light and in turn we are not supposed to hide the light in a bushel but rather we should be casting that light in all directions in this world. The only way that we can reflect the image of God into the lives of others is through reflecting God's idea of love in our own lives. Love shown toward family and those close to us can only be noticed by the outside world. The Bible says: "A new command I give to you, that you love one another as I have loved you, that you also love one another. By this shall all men know that you are my disciples, if you have love one to another." The world will look at the way you love each other to see the type of love God expects them to have for each other. Believer's love for each other is to be the model to the unbelieving world of how they should love each other.

God loves us personally—fulfilling our one-dimensional needs. God loves us powerfully—fulfilling our two-dimensional need to feel empowered, special or honored. God loves us passionately—fulfilling our three-dimensional need to be loved mind, body and soul. God loves us permanently and perfectly beyond our sin, beyond our needs, exceeding our wants, beyond our fears, beyond our judgments with no conditions attached. Jesus said, love one another as I have loved you and greater love hath no man than this; that a man lay down his life for his friends. We love because He first loved us. The key to giving love is to first receive love from him. The secret to loving right is living loved. Live as though you are loved with esteem that is built on God's love for you. You are worthy of all the love that God shows to you, and you are worthy to be loved in the very same way by those in your life.

Hugh Harmon

8.

Worthy to receive His love

Herein is love, not that we loved God, but that he loved us.
1 John 4:10

God loves you and there is nothing that you can do about it! He may not like what you are doing, and He may not like some of the things that you say to each other in the name of love but He still loves you. That is a love that by our human standards is difficult to comprehend. In this chapter I would like to delve further into the subject of God's idea of love. I don't profess to know all that there is to know about love by God's standards but I do know that what I knew prior to becoming a born again believer is far less than what I now know. This is both as a result of my understanding of salvation, and because of my life experience in the name of love. How many of you would agree that love could carry you places, both literally and figuratively? How many of you would also agree that there is as much to learn from mistakes, as there is to learn from success?

In the gospel of St. Luke the seventh chapter there is a story of a woman. A woman who has since become a pivotal figure, even a figure of controversy with respect to her relationship to Jesus. This woman has come to be known as one of the Mary's in the Bible, despite some theological debate over that fact, but more essential than her identity is the illustration that is presented in her encounter with Jesus in the chapter. Some have called her a prostitute, or a woman of ill-repute but in general we can agree that she was considered less than desirable company for Jesus Christ. A man of such stature, with disciples, speaking prophetically, preaching and teaching the word of God with an authority that surpassed even the scribes of his day should never be associating himself with a woman of this stature or dubious reputation, should he?

The Bible never really goes into detail as to how she got into the lifestyle that she was in but we could figure that her reputation in the community was far less than stellar. He reputation preceded her. She probably worked under the cover of darkness. She was also probably very careful in how she carried out her business. She most likely only dealt with strangers or people of her lower caste. Regardless of all the negatives attached to this woman Jesus counted her worthy enough to come to her defense in the face of scathing public accusation and insult, and show her love.

Let us examine what led up to this encounter, because a study of the pro-text and post-text of this incident will give us a clear, and eye-opening look at the context of the story. Just prior to this house visit Jesus is actually preaching about unbelief. He scolds the scribes and Pharisees with the fact that they really have no focus in their belief. He compares them to fickle children, who are easily distracted and are unfocused in what they really want.

In Luke 7:33 Jesus reminds them that John the Baptist came, not eating, not drinking and they called him a devil. He goes on to say that he comes along eating and drinking and they call him a glutton and a drunk, a friend of sinners, still of the devil. But these Pharisees didn't understand that Jesus' love was carrying him places. They didn't understand that His love was meant to go to the heart of sinners and not just saints. Jesus' love carried him into the presence and into the company of sinners because they are the ones to whom He came to minister salvation. And salvation is only worthwhile to the one that needs saving.

The Bible says that Christ Jesus came into the world to save sinners and Jesus himself said that he came not to call the righteous to salvation but sinners to repentance. A life vest is deemed important only when it is flung to the rescue of someone who is drowning. A great swimmer in calm, level waters needs no life vest. Jesus was trying to let these men see that their focus on the imperfections of others had allowed them to miss the whole purpose of his ministry. It is because you are imperfect that Jesus Christ counts you worthy of receiving his perfecting power and love.

Following this exchange we see Jesus entering the house of a Pharisee who had invited him to come and dine. Jesus could have easily rejected the invite and may have been right in doing so. He could have brought up the fact of the Pharisees stiff-necked attitude just a few verses earlier, and he also could have considered that the Pharisees constituted the greatest opposition to his ministry. However, Jesus never being one to let an opportunity to teach or plant a seed into someone's life conceded, and accepted the invitation. We see here that Jesus was allowing his love to carry him even into an area that others might consider almost dangerous to his reputation. Jesus in doing what he did taught us a lesson in that love should overstep our personal inhibitions. From a personal point of view we can be honest if it were up to us, being in the position that Jesus was in, and given his relationship with the Pharisees we would have avoided them at all cost. However, Jesus Christ was not like us especially in his thoughts.

There is a saying that discretion is the better part of valor. In exhibiting bravery or courage it is better to be discreet because discretion shows that you are thinking, reasoning with common sense. But would you believe that God's love isn't always discreet. And we can't always attach the moniker of common sense to what God renders as love. Common sense as we know it is derived or contrived from limited human intelligence or knowledge. But God is omniscient and Jesus Christ in showing love did not show love according to his own human feelings but rather operated according to the will of God in all that he did. The Bible does say abstain from all appearance of evil. But it doesn't say do that and cost someone spite or at the cost of showing love.

As far as the Pharisees and the others gathered at this man's house thought Jesus was indulging in evil by just associating with this woman. In their eyes he could have been more discreet not necessarily in his encounter with her but more so in the pleasure that he felt at what she had done. Both Jesus and the woman could have been a little more tactful in their approach in the opinion of these people gathered at this house.

Human love that does not carry you beyond yourself is probably not love at all. Love isn't always discreet. God's love for you isn't discreet. He kept you breathing, seeing, and hearing, in health and in strength even when you were living in rebellion and in opposition to Him. He kept you indiscreetly even when you did not want to be kept.

If the crippled man on the bed of affliction and especially his friends had been a little more discreet he probably would have never been healed. But they pushed pass discretion, tore the roof off the hut and carried their friend into the presence of the healer. It was their faith fueled by love that took them to those extremes. If the woman with the issue of blood had been more discreet she would probably have died with that issue of blood. But she indiscreetly pushed through the crowd and crawled until she could just reach the hem of Jesus' garment. She crawled on her hands and knees so that she could make contact with His love.

Humans are inherently selfish. We do things most of the time that would be of benefit to us. We account wisdom to the value with which it affects us. We love wisely most of the time. We seek out mates after we get some data about them. We seek out relationships based on the information we have gathered. Some of us gather erroneous information and that curtails the wisdom of our choice and some of us choose to ignore information and that also hinders the wisdom of our choices. But again the wisdom of God's love goes beyond what we count as wise and can even seem strange or foolish. The Bible does say that God takes the foolish things to confound the wise. He says love your enemies. How wise in our eyes is that?

What wisdom was there in Jesus indulging this prostitute to anoint his feet with valuable oil? And then in Him actually showing appreciation for it? Jesus could have dismissed her action and scolded her as ably as the others in the room had already done in their hearts.

They had all nobler suggestions or so they thought- what a waste of good oil, the money that they could get for that oil could buy food for five poor families in the community. That is what wisdom told them. That would be a wise show of love. How wise was it of her to spill her entire box of oil? She was spilling all that was of any monetary value to her on this man's foot.

Love overwhelmed her. She was no longer thinking straight and wisely. She no longer had to think wisely, she had grasped that wisdom was at her fingertips and she was going to bless him for changing her life around. I believe that this woman had been following Jesus for quite some time and just wanted an opportunity to repay his kind words. It was not longer a matter of wisdom but just pure love.

Think of your life, how wise a decision was it to get saved and join a crazy family like a church family? How wise is it that you shout, dance and praise God when everything in your sight is falling apart? How wise it that you just wait, and see the salvation of the Lord? How wise is it to love God despite losing your child, parent, or husband to a deadly disease? Or divorce? How wise was it for you to leave the office smiling after getting a pink slip when you just purchased a new house? In the eyes of man you are nothing short of a fool. But in the eyes of God you have made the wisest choice yet. Unwise love can take you out of the pit of hell and into the path of heaven.

Was what the woman did calculated, or planned? Was Jesus' response to her also planned, or thought out meticulously? We aren't given any background into that exchange or those facts but we do know that by the look of things they probably weren't on either part. What the woman did from her point of view just happened? I'm sure that she didn't plan to pour on his feet only but that is what happened. Her uncalculated show of love worked. And His unplanned response born out of his inability to be nothing anything less than honest was to show her love back.

Oftentimes it is the love that we plan that is the love that is not returned. Have you ever been carried away to do something for a loved one outside of what you considered your duty? Have you ever acted out of pure love for him or her? How about what you do for God? Do you come to church because you love God or because the Bible says you have to? Do you buy your wife gifts because you feel that you are supposed to as a husband or do you do it because you want to? Do you hug and kiss your kids because society and your pastor says that you should, or do you do it because you want to? Do you do it out of a sense of duty? What are the things that come to mind when you consider what you have ever done for God out of love and not out of duty?

The love that we show to God, and the love that we ultimately must show to each other as children of God is a love that is weighted in the worthy love that God showed us. The worthiness that is vested in us through God's love for us is of no account, if we do not expend it on others, in much the same way it is daily expended on us. Discretion, wisdom and thought are all values that are good for one to possess. But when we get into the arena of exhibiting God's love for others the love that transcends our personal hang-ups and our little idiosyncrasies we have to sometimes throw these values to the wind.

Godly love is explained in detail in the bible both from the words of Jesus and from his apostles. It is a love that is quite unlike what man has known for centuries to be love. But it is the only love that works to affect the abundant life in his kingdom. Love as we know is all about receiving but in the cardinal scripture it says For God so loved the world that He gave...and there begins the first contradiction of all that we understand to be love. The bible says that his love exceeds all things, bears all things and while all else may fail that love never fails. Lets work to make that love our love. And it begins with that scripture that says Let this mind be in you that is also in Christ Jesus. Acquiring God's love begins with mind renewal.

Love too many times is relegated to affection and warm feelings. These are not love. These pull on the strings of love because they have the nature of love in them but they are not love. Love is tender and caring that is why affection appears to be love and love does move the heart so that is why warm feelings may be mistaken for love but they are not. Affection and warm feelings are the things that we harness our hopes on when we search for love, be it in kindergarten, or at the workplace. These feelings move us to places that we many times shouldn't be. They spark lust and they spark sex outside the boundaries of marriage.

We have come to understand that love, knowing that you are loved, being loved, showing love and deliberately acting in love are primary to the realization of maturity into the abundance of God's blessings and the life that he promised. You are worthy of God's love and God is definitely worthy of your love. When I go beyond myself due to the love that is shed abroad in my heart through Christ Jesus, I become a valuable commodity in the hands of God. You can be a great value to God just as you are. God has purposed ministry in you just the way you are. God operates on purpose, by purpose and with purpose. There is a why in every what that He calls us to do.

Hugh Harmon

The Lord of hosts hath sworn saying, Surely as I have thought so shall it come to pass; and as I have purposed, so shall it stand.
Isaiah 14:24

Jesus is concerned with availability and not capability, because availability allows him to advance His purpose but capability only blocks His purpose because it puts a cap on your ability. Have you ever evoked a response in Jesus from your actions just as He responded to Mary of Bethany?

Have you ever loved God with abandonment? Forgetting what others think, forgetting protocol, forgetting how you feel, forgetting how you may be perceived and forgetting what you feel you may be in need of. How many times have you said I can't love God right now because I'm not dressed appropriately? How many times have you said I can't love God right now because I haven't been living righteously? How many times have you said in your mind that you can't love God right now because you're poor and you must be humble in my praise? Many of us believe that God is an "Indian-giver". We believe that as we have loved people and they did not reciprocate that love that so too God might do the same and not reciprocate the love we show Him.

God values love more than personal holiness. Personal holiness void of love is holi-ness, possessing holes. The problem with personal holiness is the letter "I". Holiness is spelled H-O-L-I-N-E-S-S and in the middle is the letter I. In personal holiness the letter "I" is much larger. The word, "personal" places that much more interest on the "I" in the middle. Anything personal is focused on "I". Personal holiness keeps my eye on me to see if I am white enough, or pure enough. If I talk right, if I walk right, if I look right and if I am offensive or not then I am living holy. That is what personal holiness and pursuit of it devoid of love does to us. It drives us to be so into ourselves that we can't even see ourselves as we really are.

70

Perfect love is unconcerned about how I appear or feel at the outcome. How does the love that you show add up in its ascent to perfect love? Where does love carry you? Does love carry you as far as your capabilities? Are you asking yourself, "Am I of any use?" We are not! It is never a question of being any use but of being of value to God. There is a difference between usefulness and value. Usefulness equals practicality and value denotes currency and cost. Ability or capability is not of value to God. Availability is of value to God. When we are abandoned to God, He works through us all the time. Recognize your worth in the kingdom of God and realize your status as a child of God.

9.

Abundantly loved so that we may love abundantly

**And I will very gladly spend and be spent for you; though the
more abundantly I love you, the less I be loved.**
2 Corinthians 12:15

God has shown us a love that is worth giving. The
Bible says for God so loved the world that He gave. It doesn't
say for God so loved rich people, poor people, white people,
black people, smart people or athletic people it said for God
so loved the world. The world encompasses every shape,
type and kind of people.

John 3:16 which has long been considered a
foundational truth upon which the Christian faith is based
encapsulates an abundance of meaning when it comes to the
understanding of how we must live and act as believers.
This scripture is essentially saying that God's idea of love is
directly synonymous with the idea of giving of oneself. This
scripture text was one of the first scripture verses that I
memorized as a child. I remember that in my interpretation
of the scripture I would always pay little attention to the first
clause, "For God so loved the world that He gave his only
begotten Son." My attention would always focus on the
second clause that said, "that whosoever believeth in Him
should not perish but have everlasting life." I always felt
that the most significant portion of that scripture was the
part that said if we believed we were promised life
everlasting.

However, I have since come to understand that this
scripture does not only present the imperative that we must
believe but also we must hold on to the principle that the
first clause presents. For God so loved the world he gave;
teaches us that God's great love for us led to Him giving even
more than He had already given.

For God so loved the world that He gave His only begotten Son that whosoever believeth in Him shall not perish but have everlasting life.
John 3:16

Can this scripture be telling us that the key to us loving each other correctly is that we must give more than is expected? Giving ones only begotten Son by any standards is an unexpected sacrifice for one to take. Also giving your son with the knowledge that he will have to someday give of his life to save the lives of others is an even greater level of sacrifice. In the ultimate act of love God gave His son, the essence of himself, so that He may die so that we whom He also loves may live. Jesus had to experience the mortality of life so that we may experience the immortality of eternity.

We live our lives often stumbling into an understanding of love. The thorns and thistles that we painfully encounter in our pursuit of the rose call love are usually the devices by which we crudely learn how hard true love can be. We more times than necessary learn what love is, from what we experience of what love isn't. In other words we learn more from failed love than successful love.

And I will very gladly spend and be spent for you; though the more abundantly I love you, the less I be loved.
2 Corinthians 12:15

Paul in this text talks about an abundant love that he shows toward the saints at the church at Corinth. He says that he loves them more abundantly but that love is not reciprocated; in fact he finds that the love is lessened in its return. How many of you love only to receive something in return? My love for her is predicated on the job he has and how better off I will be after we hook up. I love my parents because they buy me whatever I ask for. I love her because she's always buying me things. How deep is your love? Is it as deep as the other persons bank account or wallet?

The abundant love that God desires us to heap on each other in the Lord is a love without expectations. Paul understood this and even though he noticed his love was unrequited he still loved and loved even the more. Natural love expects something in return. This scripture says I do not care whether you love me or not. I am willing to take your degradation not for your sakes only because if it were for you I wouldn't continue to love you but rather that I may get you to God. My love is in service to God's will, not my will, but God's.

We must come to understand that God's love in me is designed to get you closer to Him. God's love in us is supposed to draw others closer to Him through me. Look at the example of Jesus Christ. The bible says that due to the grace of our Lord Jesus Christ though he was rich, yet for our sakes He became poor. God gave up glory to dwell in a human body just to be a sacrifice for our sin, for your sin and for my sin.

What are you willing to *give* up in the name of love? Are you willing to give fame and fortune, to take on indignation and shame in the name of Jesus' love for others? Are you willing to give up family and friends in the pursuit of shedding the love of God abroad and among those who most need it? Are you willing to give it all up to get the more of God?

He came to serve you and me. He came washing our feet, serving us bread and wine and healing us. When the Bible tells about the foot washing that occurred on the night of the last supper we understand that the gesture was done to the twelve. It was done to the ones who had been with Him from the very beginning, the disciples that he had been grooming for the events of that night and the days and years to follow. He washed the feet of the disciples—he cleaned probably the lowliest member of their body, the part that had the greatest contact with the dirt and dust of the earth. Their feet were dirty. But Jesus still took time to wash them. In washing the feet of his disciples, Jesus was symbolically washing the feet of all his disciples to come.

Our feet were washed the day we were saved and born again. We ate of his body (the bread) and drank of his blood (wine), the moment we asked him into our hearts, minds, bodies and lives in general. But it wasn't just washed for us, it was washed as a model for how we need to treat others. Jesus abundantly loved us so that we may abundantly give love to others.

God's idea of love is wrapped up in his condescending to love us intimately. God in essence became a servant to His own creation through His son. The idea of being a servant of God is that we serve Him by being the servants of other men. Jesus tells us in the bible that he that is greatest is not to be served but shall be the servant of all. And who was greater than Jesus in the eyes of God?

And lo a voice from heaven, saying, This is my beloved Son, in whom I am well pleased.
Matthew 3:17

Behold my servant, whom I uphold; mine elect, in whom my soul delighteth; I have put my spirit upon him: he shall bring forth judgment to the Gentiles.
Isaiah 42:1

How far are you willing to go in the service of showing God's love to others? Showing God's love may call for us to digress as another progresses. You must be willing to decrease, and do the menial so that someone else is elevated and honored. You might have to do the dirty work quietly, without getting credit for the job done. Showing God's love may be at the expense of time and energy with no material reward or compensation, just the blessing of the Lord. Showing God's love can at times and actually most times involves doing things that do not count in the estimate of men but counts a great deal in the estimate of God.

Manifesting the abundant love of God in the lives of others involves living a life of preference. We have to be ready to prefer others. The questions of what about the salary, or what about the climate, or how shall I be looked after should not be a part of our love vocabulary. These are all human considerations. Don't serve God with a reserve. When we operate in God with our eyes peeled to see if we have what it takes we will always miss the power of faith. Faith moves without seeing a way but trusting that God will make a way. Faith is the guide in the thick fog of doubt. In faith I don't leave a job to go into full time ministry just to keep a backup job on the side. If God said to leave, leave you don't need to keep some income on reserve. That shows a lack of trust in God and a lack of faith, and a lack in our love for Him.

10.

Worthy art thou to be blessed

The Spirit of the Lord God is upon me; because he hath anointed me to preach the gospel to the poor; he hath sent me to heal the brokenhearted, to preach deliverance to the captives, and recovering of sight of the blind, to set at liberty them that are bruised,

To preach the acceptable year of the Lord.

Luke 4:18,19

Jesus said these words at the beginning of his ministry in the gospel according to Luke. He says that the Spirit of the Lord was upon Him. Jesus says that this covering of the Spirit was an anointing or a consecration—a setting apart to do a specific work. Jesus proclaims that He is anointed to preach the good news of salvation. He continues to say that He was sent to heal the brokenhearted, preach deliverance to the captives—set prisoners both literally and figuratively free and recover the sight to the blind. Jesus concludes by saying that he was sent to set at liberty he who was bruised—those with hidden deep hurt.

How can you summarize this proclamation of Jesus Christ? Summarily Jesus was saying that He had come to be a blessing. A blessing is simply defined as any action that bestows upon or gives happiness to something else. It is a blessing for one to hear the good news of salvation. It is a blessing for a broken heart to be mended. It is a blessing for a captive to be given the keys to deliverance from bondage. It is a blessing for sight to be given to the blind. It is a blessing for one who is deeply hurt to be removed from that place of bruising. Now that we know that each of these proclamations was a blessing, to who was this proclamation addressed? For most of us and for many years, it has been a great stretch to think that we were counted among those being addressed.

Some years ago I adopted a personal mantra, a motto you might say that I would tell myself to encourage myself from time to time. I would stand in the mirror and repeatedly tell myself, "You are looking at someone great!" I said this over and over again until it got deep down into my spirit. This was my personal affirmation. I prayed that God would give me a wife, a life partner who would also see the greatness in me and who in turn I could share that greatness with.

Part of my personal testimony was that in my early childhood because of the circumstances under which I was raised and just because of who I was, a very introspective and personally critical individual, I struggled with the problem of low self-esteem. There are a number of other socio-economic reasons for the struggle but needless to say it was a problem, so much so that I could still remember the way I felt and even thought of myself.

I have since overcome this lack of self-esteem due to various personal achievements and because many of my then unknown gifts and talents have since been nurtured to maturity. But stemming from this battle to overcome the lack in self-dignity and esteem I purposed that I was going to encourage myself. I think that you too should adopt a mantra of your own. You may not have the same struggle that I had. You may have always had a healthy perception of self, but there may be other areas or issues that you know that you struggle with. Go to God and find out where your lack is or where it is that there is some confusion, some question in your mind as to whether your thinking on it is correct. Then let God give a personal self-affirmation. It is a powerful way to access a blessing from the Lord especially when you feel that all around you are against you. David said that he had to encourage himself in the Lord when the people were out for his blood. So do it now, you can even borrow mine, just for now. Look into the mirror and say to yourself, "Your are looking at someone great!"

Thus far, throughout this book, we have looked at many of the ways that we can come into a place of understanding first God's worth to us and subsequently our worth to Him in the furtherance of His kingdom work here on earth. In this chapter, I think that we should re-examine the issue of our position in Christ versus our condition in the flesh. It is great that we are coming to a better understanding of our worth but if we still fall trap to the weakness of our flesh we are still no better off than when we started this journey. Knowledge of a thing may give you an awareness of it but it does not guarantee that you will not be subject to its entrapments. It takes knowledge, planning and action to overcome. We are overcome when we passively let the floods envelop our heads, but we become overcomers when we actively swim above the current and the flood.

The first step we take in establishing a firm foundation in our lives is when we realize who we are, and not only this but also whose we are. It is when we come to a place of recognizing our self-worth that we can surely soar. There is a well-known saying that claims that there are three kinds of people in the world:
1. Those who make things happen.
2. Those who watch things happen.
3. Those who wonder what happened.
We know that from this saying it is encouraged that you should align or strive to be affixed among the type 1 people—those who make things happen.

If we did a survey of any given room of people in any given setting we quite possibly may find a large fraction of the people in the room consider themselves as movers and shakers. However, self-perception does not make a world-changer be. It is also inevitable, and clear just because of the established order of things that all of us cannot occupy the realm of motivator because then there would be no one to motivate. Inherently some of us will be those who watch things happen, and those who wonder what happened. Especially if you are the type that have no problem minding your own business you will be wondering what happened quite often.

From a spiritual point of view, with regard to the composition of the body of Church we are faced with a similar trichotomy of people:
1. Those who know their place in Christ.
2. Those who don't know their place in Christ.
3. Those who don't have a clue that such a place existed.

Unfortunately if we would be honest many of us would unlike the other categories find ourselves disproportionately occupying group three; those who don't have a clue that there was such a place in Christ.

The problem of sin sick believers is the problem of the lack of understanding of their position in Christ. The problem of the backslider is not the problem of falling out of fellowship with the body of Christ but rather it is the problem of ignorance of being a viable necessary part of that body. Saints fall into sin because they are unaware of the value of their inheritance after they have said, "I do" to Jesus in salvation. People backslide because they fail to see the significance of their role in the body of Christ or the magnitude of their obligation to Christ. Are you obliged to stay in God's will or are you obliged to assume the mandates of your condition?

My Bishop, Kenneth Moales, Sr., once said that some people are going to hell not because of sin, but because they have a problem that they won't let God solve for them. Sin isn't the problem; it is choosing to abide in sin that is the problem. Jesus Christ conquered sin and death on the Cross and gave you the gift of salvation so why are you taking up that dead thing again. You have a problem of being attracted to dead things...dead men, dead women, dead business associates, dead jobs, dead relationships, dead ways via even more deceased means.

Just a few years ago some of us who are now saved were type "A" sinners. We were servants of sin as Jesus said in John 8:34. We were on the verge of dying in our sin. Some of us were slaves to lust, lasciviousness, engaged in all manner of evil. But one day, the carpenter came along offering us not only an opportunity to get our crooked paths straight but offering us life not just mere long life but abundant life. He came along and offered us an apprenticeship, working in his house, out of his workshop with free access to his tools. He didn't just give us another chance, and some more time. He gave us access to eternity.

2 Timothy 1:9 says that he hath saved us and called us with a holy calling, not according to our works, but according to his own purpose and grace. At that moment, at that time when Jesus applied the medication to cure the cancer of death that had enveloped us we recognized what we were. We knew we were sinners; we had an Adam and Eve experience and knew that we were as it was naked, and bare, less than perfect. Some of us were perfected in sin. Which is essentially being perfectly broken.

We recognized that the gap between God, and ourselves was vast. We confessed our sins to God eager for Him to give us a remedy to what was ailing us. Be careful that you don't let the desire for a quick cure or relief of pain is your motivation for seeking salvation. Did you accept salvation as a ticket to easy street? Or did you get saved because in your heart you knew that you had a sin problem?

We realized that we could never be god, or even little gods. Beware of the little god complex. You were made first of all, that means you had a beginning. Second you were made in his image, not as an exact carbon copy, that means you lack the essence of His omnipotence. You were made for his divine purposes and not your own, God operates out of his own volition. We were saved and baptized in Jesus name. We understood that we now had to observe all of Christ's commandments. As Matthew 28:20 says: Teaching them to observe all things whatsoever I have commanded you; and lo, I am with you always even unto the end o the world! The 'them' in this scripture refers to us.

Many of us saved, sanctified as we are, actually are living unaware of our privilege. We are living either in group 2 or 3—those who don't know what their place is in Christ and those who didn't even know that there was such a place. Many of us are quite aware of our condition, but we are conversely unaware of our position in Him.

Position vs. Condition: Place vs. Posture, Prognosis vs.

Diagnosis

How many of you have ever felt as if you don't really know where you are? Have you ever been lost? Have you ever been physically lost but spiritually sure that you would find your way back on the right path? What does it mean to be lost? It simply means that you are heading in a given direction to a decided location but your present location is unfamiliar and you are not sure in which direction you should be heading. Have you ever found yourself in a position of leadership but with a condition of ill health? Have you ever-experienced victory but have the after affects of pain--a sense of regret for the hurt that you have experienced in the name of pursuit of victory? A marathon runner would be familiar with what I am talking about. Paul the Apostle said that the race is not for the swift but for him that endures to the end. Endurance isn't easy it is energy consuming and painful. My position in Christ is a real place, my condition in this flesh is a real feeling but God's purpose for me is even more real.

In Genesis 1:26 it says that God made man in His image. We were created not physically like God because God is a spirit. However, we are spirit beings as He is but housed in human flesh. Our essential parts although imperfectly tainted by sin, finite and cloaked in mortal flesh we have and can attain his communicable attributes. God's communicable attributes include life in Him, his personality, his godly truth, his wisdom, his love, his holiness and his justice. It is because of these godly characteristics that we can fellowship with God in the spirit. In this scripture text in Genesis we are made privy to a heavenly board meeting. And God says to God, "Let us make man in our image...this is our first glance, our first delineation of our original position, of our original posture, our original rank and our original status.

Our original position was a place of rule, a place of dominion. But just a few chapters later we see the arrival, consequence and penalty of sin. One of which was the usurping of dominion and rule from man to Satan. Man was hoodwinked, and bamboozled by the enemy, Satan. God gave man a mandate to be fruitful, multiply and subdue the earth both the land and all that dwelt therein. The serpent was counted among that which man was to subdue and rule over. But with subtleties the enemy usurped that power from man's hands, simply by the act of suggestive thinking and lies.

Hebrews 2:8 support this understanding of the coup d'etats that the devil caused against man.

Thou hast put all things in subjection under his feet. For in that he put all in subjection under him, he left nothing that is not put under him. But now we see not yet all things put under him.
                                    Hebrews 2:8

So we see man's original position was dominion and rule, he fell and Jesus came to die that we may be restored to dominion and rule. So there stands the latitude of our position.

What about man's condition?

My condition is my state of being. My condition is my state of fitness or my state of health. What was God's original intent for my condition? We find out that man's condition in the same book of Genesis in Chapter 2 verse 7. God formed man of the dust of the ground. We were fashioned from the dust; we were earthy of simple form. Our condition, our state of being was corruptible, spoilable, less than the perfect God that had created us. Our condition was our susceptibility to sin. We were not sinful but we had free will. That gave us the option to choose sin. God in his perfection was unable to sin, we on the other hand were able to sin. Our original position was dominion, and our original condition was corruptible, with the ability to sin.

How is it that we had position of power but yet still had such condition of sin? In order to understand the dichotomy presented in our existence, we must spotlight our place. God made us from dust. He inculcated or placed his communicable attributes in us. He assigned us a position. We possessed an inherent condition. God has certain expectations of us.

How can we control our condition enough to correctly operate in our position? When we address this topic we are dealing with four factors: our eternal position, our physical/essential condition, God's expectation of us, and God's remedy for us if we fall short of his expectations.

According as he hath chosen us in him before the foundation of the world, that we should be holy and without blame before him in love:
Ephesians 1:4

This scripture tells us that we were chosen in Him before the foundation of the world. This speaks of our position—chosen by the Highest, set for promotion, designated as one to be groomed for a high place. It continues to say that we should be holy and without blame before him in love—this speaks of expectation. God wants holiness.

The bible is riddled through with God's expectation of holiness from his people. 1 Peter 1:15,16 implores us to be holy for He is holy. Hebrews 12:14 says, "Follow peace with all men, and holiness without which no man shall see the Lord."

What is being holy? Is holiness perfection? Can man attain true holiness? Webster's dictionary defines holiness as the quality of spiritual purity, living in absolute devotion, or simply sacred. Perfection however, is defined as being without fault or defect. All men have fallen short of perfection but any man can live holy. Holiness is an attainable goal or expectation. It calls for absolute truth, complete honesty, wisdom, love and justice. There were many men and women who lived holy in the eyes of God both in the biblical times and even during this present time. These men were not perfect as we know perfection to be but they were holy.

Moses wasn't perfect—he had a speech impediment, and was murderer by our standards. He was on occasion swift to wrath but he lived so holy that God communed with Him one on one. God communicated his law and commandments to him personally, dare say face to face. The proximity within which Moses came into the presence of the Lord is a testimony to the level of holiness by which he had to be living.

Samuel the Prophet wasn't perfect but he lived holy. Samuel's lack of perfection showed through in the way that he raised his children. They grew up to walk in the way of sin, taking bribes and perverting the judgment as priest of the temple. However, Samuel was given the commission of anointing the Kings of Israel, of being the mouthpiece of the Lord. Peter, the apostle, the rock on which Christ built his church wasn't perfect but after being imbued with the Holy Spirit he lived holy. Paul, the apostle, the Christian persecutor was far from perfect but became a great teacher on the principles of holy living.

How can I a simple man, without ever having experienced a personal face to face encounter with God, without having walked with him, without having personally witnessed his miracles first hand? How can I really live up to His expectations, take advantage of my position and still deal with my human condition? Our frailties, our weaknesses, our handicaps, the seeming strongholds that are constantly before us, those things that keep us in prayer, seeking his grace and his mercy all have solutions locked up in Him. In Him, through Him and by Him we live, move and have our being. It is in Him we are positioned through salvation, it is of him that we were made predisposed to our condition, and it is through Him we can overcome this condition.

Jesus revealed to us the mechanism by which our condition is redeemed. After the fall our position of rule and dominion was ruptured, our frail condition caused sin to fester in us. God in his grand purpose sought to restore us to our original state and to deal with the cancer of sin. Cancer stems from a malignant tumor. This tumor tends to spread in the body. It corrodes slowly and fatally. A tumor is just a mass of tissue or group of cells, familiar cells that are dysfunctional but can only do what is innate and that is to multiply. Divide and separate aimlessly that is their function. This is how sin works in our flesh. Your flesh accepts sin and lets it fester because your flesh is familiar with it. In order for one to stop cancer you have to halt its reproduction or growth. This is where chemotherapy comes into play, when powerful chemicals are applied to the affected area. Why does chemotherapy work? It works because of the potency or the power of the chemicals.

Jesus said in Luke 24:49
And behold I send the promise of my Father upon you: but tarry ye in the city of Jerusalem, until ye be endued with power from on high.

St. John 1:12 says:
But as many as received him, to them gave he power to become sons of God even to them that believe on his name.

In Matthew 28:18 Jesus says:
All power is given unto me in heaven and in earth.

Again we see the source of the remedy, Jesus. I am with you always, even unto the end of the world. The Holy Spirit gives us power to overcome our condition and move back into our rightful position. But our power is useless if we do not use it. A V6 Chevy Impala parked with its engine off on I-95 can't beat a 4 cylinder Hyundai Elantra moving at 60 mph on the same I-95. The Chevy has more power in its engine but its power is inactive. There are too many saints sitting up in church with power on the inside but it is not evident in their walk. They have power on the inside while on their jobs, while at school, while spending time with family but that power is not manifested as readily as it should. That is why spiritual cancer is so prevalent. That is why we have infected saints knowing that they have power but also unaware that unattended sin is slowly killing them. Many people who have cancer don't realize it until it is too late. Cancer can be a slow, silent killer. Too many saints mired in sin feeling that it is just something that they have to go through and constantly repent from. We have too long accepted falling, failing and succumbing to sin as part of life.

There are tools at our disposal to pull us free of this bondage. Repetitive sin and repentance is not what God expects. Think of our situation as of an automobile, the engine is your spirit. The fuel is the power of the Holy Spirit. The drive is our faith: when we put the engine in drive with belief and action coupled with expectation. The oil is prayer, praise, and worship. This keeps the engine well lubricated. The mechanic is your or a Pastor, the man of God that repairs through the Word and the laying on of hands. The repair shop is the church where fellowship of the saints occurs.

I now know that I have a place or position in Christ that is above any position that I could attain in the world. I now know that I am numbered among the group that makes things happen. I now know that I have power.

2 Timothy 2:21 says that if we purge ourselves we will become as vessels of honor sanctified, fit for the master's use. With power we can flee lust, follow righteousness, peace, faith and charity.

When I was trying to find a scripture that fully summarized the concept of our position vs. our condition, I was drawn to the account in Zechariah 3. The prophet Zechariah has a vision of the high priest Joshua and in the vision Zechariah is made witness to what I like to call the Joshua experience.

Joshua the high priest called of God, standing before God with Satan at his right hand to resist him. Who is Joshua? "I am Joshua, you are Joshua we are Joshua!"

> **But ye are a chosen generation, a royal priesthood, an holy nation, a peculiar people; that ye should shew forth the praise of him who hath called you out of darkness into this marvelous light.**
> **1 Peter 2:9**

We are as priest standing before the Lord with Satan at our right hand to resist us. Satan is standing in our symbolic place of power but he has no power but what we

88

give to him. God looks upon us and sees Satan and rebukes Him on our behalf and states that he knows our condition, a brand plucked from the fire. A brand saved from the destined place of sin, hell. God plucked us out of the path of sin and death.

Joshua was clothed in filthy rags and stood before the angel. We are clothed in filthy rags and stand before our angel, Pastor Hezekiah Walker. And the Lord tells Pastor to take away our filthy rags. Preach deliverance to our souls and bring us out of the cloak of sin. Remove our grave clothes. And I will clothe thee with a change of raiment. God will clothe us in fine linen, place a crown, a miter upon our heads. We were high priest (that was great), we had power, but now God is making us into kings and judges with authority to rule over his house. He is making us into the greater. Get ready for the greater.

11.

Worthy Art Thou to live and not die

And when I passed by thee, and saw thee polluted in thine own blood, I said unto thee when thou wast in thy blood, Live; yea, I said unto thee when thou wast in thy blood, Live.
Ezekiel 16:6

In this chapter I want to declare to you that God said, "Live!" The bills are late, the rent is due, the car note is overdue, your insurance has lapsed but God says, "Live!" Your wife wants a divorce, your husband just walked out with another woman, and you just lost your job. But God says, "Live!" He came home drunk last night and you're bruised and battered this morning but God says, "Live!" You just found out that you're pregnant, and you're not married, and he doesn't want anything to do with you and God says, "Live!" Maybe it's not that bleak. Probably you are a born again believer and you've been praying for deliverance but you're still feeling the pain. You've been praying for prosperity but you're still seeing poverty. You've been praying for power and you're still feeling weak but God says, "Live!" I would like to ask you a simple question, "Are you ready to live?"

When we consider the question of our readiness to experience the God ordained type of love, there are a few other questions that come to mind. Questions such as: Am I really living? Am I living as I should? Am I doing the things day and day out that qualify as what God would consider as living? Or am I really just dying? We have to understand that life can be one of two very distinct experiences. It could be a daily taste of the abundance of a God sustained walk, or it could be a daily march toward a sure physical demise. Which one are you doing? Along which path is the imprint of your footstep making its impression?

Are you living to live again or are you living like there is nothing after this? Living with no concept of the life giver, being nothing more than a life taker. There is a thin line between living and dying and that thin line is the one that separates the sinner from the saint and the saved from the insane. Many of us would agree that real life, real living; the concrete experience of vitality is something that we all desire in our time here on earth.

The bible says that it is appointed man once to die and after that judgment. But before death and before judgment we can agree that we want to know how we should live. Many times we go through this world, this life, this existence with one thing on our minds and that is how not to die.

We equip our surroundings and ourselves with devices to ensure our safety and protection, things that profess to keep us hidden or protected from the possibility of death but we seldom really seek out things that give us life. We look for ways to live longer to hide the fact that we are getting closer to death, we seek the fountain of youth, we take pills that claim to make one live longer but we never really live. And God says, "Live!"

The misunderstanding of the essence of life stems from the erroneous definitions we have of life. We believe that to live is simply the act of preventing death. Life is defined as the property of animals and plants that makes it possible for them to take in food, to get energy and to grow. Therefore in other words life in the natural is the ability to eat, be energized and to grow. But what is life in the spiritual? What is life from God's perspective? What does God mean when God says, "Live!"

To understand God's definition of life we must go back to the examples of how God spoke or ordained life into others. As I began to investigate the idea of life from God's perspective I was led to a scripture in the book of the prophet Ezekiel. In the 16th chapter of Ezekiel we are given an illustration of the prophet speaking prophetically about life. Ezekiel is speaking here in a voice that is reminiscent of one who is merely a mouthpiece of the Almighty. In essence it is God speaking about his relationship with the people of Israel. And here in the foundational text beginning at the 4th verse we here God speaking through the mouth of the prophet and saying, "I saw you laying in your own blood as I passed by and I said, "Live!" God says at your birth, at your beginning, at your start...I saw. It's one thing to be going through a rough time in life, to be experiencing abuse, to be in constant fear and under pressure and feel that no one knows and that no one sees and that no one cares. As the song goes, "Nobody knows the trouble I see..." However God says that he saw from the day of your birth. He saw how you were unwanted, how you were a castaway and how you were not appreciated.

Some of us started out in circumstances that were less than good. We sought life first at home, from family and friends. We entered this world screaming and kicking, we expected to find life in the one's closest to us. But what if the ones closest to us lack life. We grow up looking for life in friends, in the things that we do, in the things that we possess, in the places that we go, in the contacts and the circles that we run in. But what if these people, these things, these places, these contacts too lack life.

Our self-esteem is shot our self-image is twisted, we think of ourselves as nothing more than what others think of us. Where do we go, what do we seek, who do we look to for this real life? Disillusioned you settle for thinking that your lot is to eat, drink and be merry for tomorrow you will die. Ezekiel 16:5 says in the New International Version translation of the Bible, "No one looked on you with pity or had compassion enough to do any of these things for you. Rather, you were thrown out into the open field, for on the day you were born you were despised." And verse 6 says, "Then I passed by..."

In your mind prior to God passing by there was no chance, prior to that saint speaking a Word into your life, or that preacher prophesying over your situation or that encouraging smile. Even after that encouraging gesture from that person on the job that you thought had no idea, you thought that there was no chance for you. You thought how could this twisted life be made right? You thought how can I be lifted out of this mess of an existence and be made clean?

Son of man, can these bones live?
Ezekiel 37:3

God wants us to understand that regardless of the bumps, bruises, the darkness that is all around us when he says, "Live!" it is bound to happen. Proverbs 4:20 says Give attention to my words; incline your ear to my sayings. Do not let them depart from your eyes; keep them in the midst of your heart; for they are life to those who find them and health to all their flesh. God says life is in my word. When you hear it you have life. When you see His word you have life. When you keep His word in your heart you have life. When you treasure his word you have life and you have health in your flesh.

This goes out to those who have come to a realization either some years ago or maybe even just recently that without Jesus you would be dead. I'm speaking to someone who was almost aborted someone who was born but left for dead, one who was used and abused. This is for those who were beaten and bloody and left scarred and bruised and who were told that they would never be anything. The single mother, left to raise the children alone, young unskilled, unemployed and abandoned by your own family, still a child but God still says, "Live!" God's request for us to live is not limited to those who are experiencing the bliss of peace, joy and love. It is extended to the rejected, downtrodden and less than fortunate. God says, live to the abused young girl who feels like she wants to die. He says live to the young boy who is confused about what it is to be a man because every image that he has had of men in his life have been images that are far less than flattering. God says live to the father who has always run away from his problems and to the mother who blames the "good-for-nothing" father for her troubles.

We live in a time and an age when people are desperate to live. To live is synonymous today with being in the mix, involved in the things that everyone else is doing. Living is defined today as being counted among the number. These new conceptions of what life is can create real challenges for people like the ones mentioned earlier, those who seem to have all the cards stacked against them. The negative cards of early childhood abuse, divorce, infidelity and poor self-image all throw a monkey wrench in any of these groups attempts to fit in and live. We consider ourselves to be living if we are involved in the hustle and the bustle of everyday activity. If we are moving at a fast pace on our jobs, making connections and going up the corporate ladder we are living by contemporary standards. Signs of life today are financial prosperity and ones ability to afford the finer things. We are considered to be living if we don't let the world pass us by. This resolute stance of having to be constantly changing with the trends of the world around us is just plain nonsensical. If you stick and move, and rip and run and stand for nothing and fall for anything and chase after everything you will just be taking steps toward dying. Much of what we really seek after in the name of life is actually bringing us death.

World famous designer Cocoa Chanel once said that in order for one to be irreplaceable one must always be different. In my opinion being different does not mean to be always changing but rather it means that one must choose to live by a resolute standard. One must choose to drink from the fountain of life or choose to dig wells or cisterns to gather the falling rain, it's all about the source.

For my people have committee two evils; they have forsaken me the fountain of living waters, and hewed them out cisterns, broken cisterns that can hold no water.
Jeremiah 2:13

To understand what life is we must understand where life begins. Ezekiel 37 says that God shall put his spirit in you and you shall live. God begins the process. He is the source of life. The Bible speaks repeatedly of God's faithfulness. It speaks of his compassion, of his desire to see us prosper, of his desire to see us live. Regardless of our beginning, our lows, or the darkness that we have to endure God says that he comes to give us a new end, he comes to lift us above our former state. He comes to bring us into the light of his righteousness.

God is a faithful God who keeps covenant and mercy for a thousand generations with those who love Him and keep His commandments.
Deuteronomy 7:9

God says live but where should we look for life. The prophet Ezekiel says that God shall put his spirit in you and you shall live. God begins the process. In order for you to live you must recognize the life source. God says live because he is providing the substance of what he requests of you to live. God will provide the "just enough" that you need in order to live. The Bible says that Jesus is the resurrection and the life, he wants to resurrect your messed up situation and give you life. It says that He is the way, the truth and the life and every man that comes unto him shall surely come unto the Father.

What must I do to live? In order for life to enter, death must take an exit. The Bible says what communion hath light with darkness. The first day that we spend in this physical life, is the first step that we take to physical death. So God is saying that physical life is not what I am talking about. To live life seeking the physical things such as money, friends, influence, power, fame and prestige without first seeking Him is like committing suicide. It is in truth living in death.

In order to live you must kill worldly lust, worldly habits, and deceit in your heart. In order to live you must actively pursue holiness and godliness in your lives.

> **Brethren, I count not myself to have apprehended: but this one thing I do, forgetting those things which are behind (forgetting the former things) and reaching forth unto those things which are before. I press toward the mark for the prize of the high calling of God in Christ Jesus.**
> **Philippians 3:13**

Life begins with salvation but it does not stay with it. Next comes sanctification and deliverance. It is in these steps that we experience life and that everlasting. God says come as you are, dying, bloodied and bruised and I will give you rest. He says I will not only heal you of your afflictions but I shall also give you a fresh start. We are coming to church bloody. We are coming bruised and vexed with our worldly conditions. We are wallowing in our own blood and looking for sympathy from God. We are hurt and untrustworthy of everyone around us. We don't know whom to trust. We don't want to open up to God just in case He doesn't care like everyone else. We look at God like we look at men and we rate his love and compassion on a human scale. We compare Him to the losers for lovers that we've always had, and the lying deceivers that we recently ran into. But God is faithful and just. Our life might not be fair but God is surely just.

> **Jesus died so that we that live should not live for ourselves but live unto Jesus who died for us.**
> **2 Corinthians 5:15**

God is saying don't close up and die alone, open up and live with Him. In other words we are covered and delivered and delivered to recover. He covered us in His blood, replacing our blood. We are saved to save another. This life that Jesus expects of us is a life of J.O.Y., Jesus first, Others second and Yourself last. God said live not just for you, but for everybody connected to you.

For none of us liveth to himself, for whether we live, we live unto the Lord;
Romans 14:7,8

12.

Worthy Art Thou to choose

And he said unto Jesus, Lord, remember me when thou comest into thy kingdom.
And Jesus said unto him, Verily I say unto thee, To-day shalt thou be with me in paradise.

Luke 23: 42

This life that we live is riddled with choices. The things that we experience from day to day are intricately tied to the choices that we make. You make a choice each and every day as to whether you will make it out to your job or not. You make a choice as to whether you will praise the Lord. You make choices when it comes to worship and when it comes to living according to His will or your own will. You make choices.

The fact that you make choices suggests that you have choices. The choices you make given the circumstances you face determine the man and the woman that you will become. Wisdom is a choice. Living, acting and even speaking wisely are daily choices that we make. As long as there is more than one option available to us we have a choice. Our choices are limited by our ignorance. The more knowledge we have of a thing the greater the choices we have with regard to how we tackle that thing.

The world sometimes suggests that there are situations in which we have no choice. We are taught in those cases that we must do what we have to do. But in my opinion even the sentiment of having to do what you have to do is in itself a choice. What are the roots of the choices that we have? How does the topic of our worth in the eyes of God relate to the choices that we are empowered with through Him? The question is did we always have a choice?

To answer the question of whether we always had a choice I would have to say, no. In the beginning God created heaven and He created earth. He created plants, vegetation, animals and He planted a garden. It was after these things were put into place that God created man and He put man in the garden. Adam had no choice in how he was to be formed, God simply said, "Let us make man in our image..." God made man as He pleased. Adam had no choice in where he was to begin life. God did not consult with his creation he consulted with himself. Adam had no choice in what gender he was to be.

We are very much like Adam the first man. We also have no choice in where we are born. We have no choice in what form we will take. We have no choice in our gender. We have no choice in who our parents will be. We have no choice in whether we will be born into poverty or into wealth. We have no choice in the assignment of siblings, or race. So when and where does choice come into play? When and where did choice come into play in the life of Adam?

And the Lord God commanded the man, saying of every tree of the garden thou mayest freely eat: But of the tree of the knowledge of good and evil, thou shalt not eat of it; for in the day that thou eatest thereof thou shalt surely die.
Genesis 2:16,17

We look at this scripture text and we see the command of God is clear but we sometimes miss the element of choice that God invites into human existence. We look at Adam and we look at God's directive and we say that Adam had no choice. He was given an ultimatum. We ask why did God put the tree there if he didn't want Adam to eat of it? Why didn't God just plant a guard around the tree to keep Adam away?

We see God as being unfair, some may even say He was tempting Adam. When we find ourselves in a place of no choices we tend to consider things to be unfair. A lack of self-determination is seen as unfair circumstances. I researched commentary on this particular incident of the introduction of the tree and some scholars have said that man's inert nature to be self-determined was part of the reason why Adam so easily disobeyed this directive. Regardless of your theological take on the incident we can conclude together that "free will" was given to Adam and every man and every woman to follow when God gave him the directive not to eat of that particular tree.

God didn't say that it is impossible for you to eat of the tree. He said, "...for in the day that thou eatest thereof thou shalt surely die." In this clause God is presenting Adam with an if. He is presenting Adam with a conditional conjunction. He is presenting Adam with an "in case that..." God establishes the fact that the consequence is irreversible. But the action that leads to the consequence of demise is still driven by choice. Adam had no choice and God had no choice with regard to the consequence that He had already established by His spoken word. God said if you eat of the tree you shall surely die. Death was already established as a condition of disobedience of this command. But God even in this warning gave Adam a choice.

Adam and Eve and there offspring were given the choice of life and death. We were given the choice to love God, to serve God and to obey God. God does not force your hand in loving Him, or in honoring Him, we choose to. Despite the myriad of choices that Adam and Eve didn't have, and the myriad of choices that we apparently don't have, we still have the choice to choose eternal life or eternal death. You have the freedom to make whatever eternal choice you desire.

In the twenty-third chapter of the book of Luke, the thirty-ninth verse we are brought to a pivotal point in Christian history. This is the point at which all our faith is validated. This is the place at which we could hang our doubts, our discouragement, our sins, and our afflictions. And this place is the cross.

In this scripture text we are introduced to the company that Jesus kept at the cross. It says that he was between two criminals. The bible refers to them more specifically as malefactors. In essence, these two other condemned men were less than desirable company for the Son of God, for royalty. These two men were eyewitnesses to the bleeding Christ. These were two men who were guilty as charged. Two men sentenced to die. Two men even though at death's doorstep still with a choice. Two men who from most accounts stood posted just an arm's length from salvation itself.

As the story goes one ridicules Jesus an asked Him, "If thou be Christ, save thyself and us." The other seeing the error in his counterpart's taunts rebukes him and reminds him that they are still at the mercy of God, and that they are also facing the same condemnation. He goes as far as to ask his fellow prisoner if he had no fear of God. We see here the drama of choice made available even to the condemned.

The Bible says that Jesus is the way, the truth and the life, and if you believe in Him you shall be saved. Here we see one man choosing not to believe in Jesus Christ. We see one man joining in the endearment of the Pharisees and Scribes and calling for Jesus to prove his claim to son ship or face the shame of dying a failure. However, we also see that one chooses to believe and in reality choose to live despite being sentenced to death. Isn't it ironic how God gives us free will even in the shadow of death? And in this free will God literally gives us freedom. He allows us to disobey. He allows us to do wrong. He allows us to choose death. Jesus allows us to freely obey. He allows us to freely love Him. He allows us to freely experience the abundant life.

Life is an accumulation of choices. Good and bad choices are part of life. Staying or leaving, better or worse, left or right, right or wrong, joy or sadness and running or standing are all choices that we have to make. We may complain about the place that we find ourselves in as a result of birth. Why did I have to be from the ghetto? Why did I have to be poor, black or white? Why did I have to have short hair, this shape or this body? Why did I have to have these parents? But beyond all these things that actually in the eyes of God's plan and his will are minor, he gives you a far greater choice, and some far more significant choices along life's way. He counts you worthy enough to give you the choice of where you spend eternity. He controls the consequence of your choice but He doesn't control your choice.

Jesus reiterated the litany of choices that God has given us from the very beginning. He said enter in at the narrow gate or the wide gate. He said travel on the narrow road or the wide road. He said build on a rock or on the sand. He said serve God or serve riches. He said be numbered among the sheep or among the goats. What if life was the other way around? What if God said you choose how you begin and I choose how you end? You choose the talent and gifts. You choose the height, weight, and physical features. You choose whether you are born into wealth or poverty. You choose high intellect and good health and let me choose whether you experience eternal life or eternal death. God gives us this all-important choice because he recognizes that we will make mistakes.

Isn't it something that you can make a life of mistakes when it come to choices, and then make one correct choice and affect a greater ending? Think of the repentant thief, we don't know much about him but we can assume he made some horrible mistakes in life. He probably chose the wrong company to be associated with. He probably had wrong morals and exhibited equally questionable behavior. But

Jesus still gave him the hand of salvation when he cried unto Him.

Is your life on course or off course? On course doesn't mean perfect. It means that even when things don't go perfectly, you are still going in the right direction. Don't let your continual bad choices seal your fate and take you off course in this life. Don't look back and say, "If only I had. If only I could." I want to say, "Yes, I can!" I might not be able to go back and make a brand new start, but I can start from now and make a brand new ending. The future doesn't get better by hoping it just looks better. It gets better by working. It's the same way with choices. It's one thing to have choices it's another thing to make these choices. Understand that Jesus loves you just as he loved that thief on the cross. He doesn't love what you are doing but he does love you and if you make the right choice today as that thief did some 2000 years ago, and even if you make the wrong choice today. God loves you enough to allow you to not choose him.

But friend I come today not to bring you false hopes or not to bring you discouragement but only to encourage you and to speak a word of hope into your life and into your situation. God doesn't care what others have labeled you, he doesn't care what the system says about you because he knows you better than anyone can, and He tells me to tell you today to choose him and he will choose you and love you the same. God loves you no less. He's no respecter of persons, if he can save me, clean me up and forgive me, He can and will do the same for you. He is not a man that he will lie, He's not double-minded, He thinks and it comes to pass, He speaks and it is made manifest. And today He speaks of your salvation in Jesus name. Amen.

About the Author

Hugh J. V. Harmon is an author, minister, teacher and motivational speaker. He's been writing full time for the past eight years and has been featured in a number of minor publications. He is a regular contributor to the Reality Check segment of the urban contemporary Christian lifestyle magazine XII (Twelve), with such feature articles as *Thirteen Faces-Chronicles from the Cage*. His first book was **Bridging the Gap**, a landmark treatise on the ministry of reconciliation. His subsequent work includes the book, **Of Gods, Giants and Icons In a world of mortals**.

Hugh's current ministry obligations include being the founder and Senior Pastor of Love Fellowship Kingdom Restoration Tabernacle of Columbia, SC. He is expanding his personal vision of a church that epitomizes the kingdom of God in the earth. Hugh is serving under the leadership and mentorship of his spiritual leader, Overseer Hezekiah Walker Jr. He is currently employed as an elementary school teacher in the Richland County, SC.

Hugh lives with his beautiful wife, Alison and daughter Chai Soleil in Columbia, South Carolina. His motto is, *"Great opportunities to do goodwill are few and far between, but small moments to make a difference through God's will are ever before us."*

Worthy Art Thou

www.ingramcontent.com/pod-product-compliance
Lightning Source LLC
Chambersburg PA
CBHW030958090426
42737CB00007B/587